KT-474-496

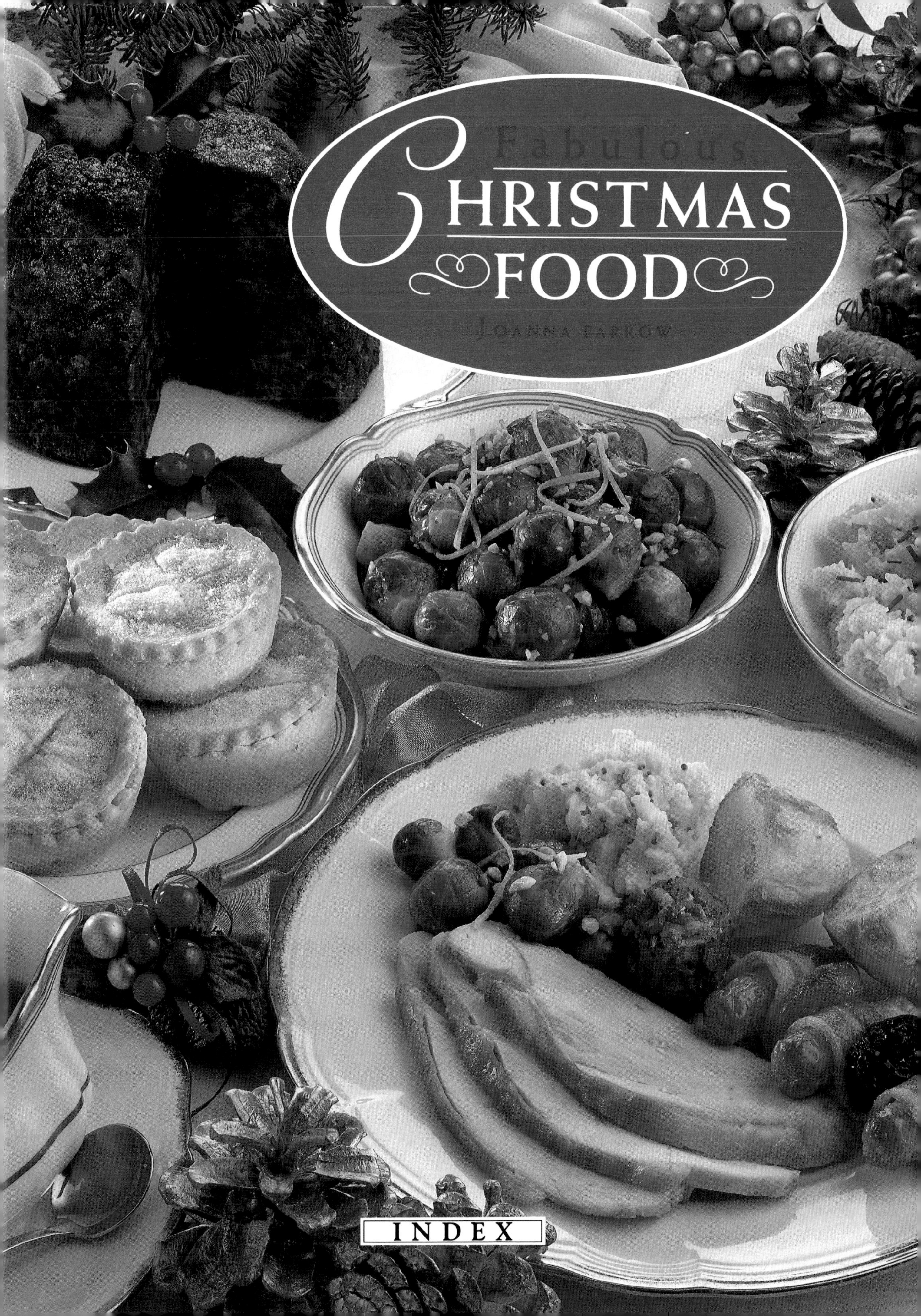
Fabulous
CHRISTMAS
FOOD
JOANNA FARROW
INDEX

CONTENTS

Published in 1996 by Merehurst Limited
Ferry House, 51–57 Lacy Road, Putney, London SW15 1PR

This edition published 1996 for INDEX
Unit 1, Garrard Way, Kettering NN16 8TD

ISBN 1 85391 642 0

A catalogue record for this book is available from the British Library

All recipes by Joanna Farrow except pp 6–9, 56–57, 62–63, 66–67, 76–79, 82–85, 89 (Peach Cup, Strawberry Cup, and Tropical Cup), and 90–93. Other recipes contributed by Maxine Clark, Carole Handslip and Lyn Rutherford.

Editor: Susanna Tee
Designer: Maggie Aldred
Photographer: Alan Marsh, except for pp 7, 9, 56–57, 62–63, 66–67, 76–79, 82–85, 89–93
Home economist: Lyn Rutherford, except for pp 7, 9, 56–57, 62–63, 66–67, 76–79, 82–85, 89–93
Stylist: Marian Price, except for pp 7, 9, 56–57, 62–63, 66–67, 76–79, 82–85, 89–93

Typesetting by J&L Composition Ltd, Filey, North Yorkshire
Colour separation by Fotographics Ltd UK – Hong Kong
Printed in Italy

Introduction

Christmas is a wonderful time for indulging in all the foods we love, and possibly the one occasion when we splash out on special treats. However, while most of us can simply look forward to the oncoming feast, there's plenty of planning and preparation for the cook. This book, with its collection of classic and unusual recipes, will make light work of the culinary arrangements for both beginners and experienced cooks.

Planning and cooking can start several weeks in advance to ease last minute pressure. First make a copious list of chosen dishes. Follow this by baking the puddings, cakes and dishes for freezing. As the big day approaches, excited children can be enlisted for making biscuits and pastries – even icing the cake.

To kick off Christmas dinner in style, serve a light starter, such as a smooth, creamy soup or pretty salad, that won't overload the cook or overfill the guests. Traditionalists can tuck into a perfectly roasted turkey with all the trimmings. For those who prefer something a little different, goose, duck and pheasant are increasingly popular alternatives. With recipes and suggestions for accompaniments, even those tackling them for the first time can do so with confidence. If fish is a firm favourite, there are several recipes, from dishes for small gatherings to a spectacular salmon and for vegetarians, an impressively festive pie. To complete the feast, there are rich puddings, iced desserts, sumptuous cakes and chocolates.

If you are planning a party over the holiday, follow the buffet ideas which focus mainly on salads or, if you have friends dropping in for drinks, the savoury nibbles. There are also delicious recipes to transform leftover food from the busy Christmas rush.

With beautifully photographed recipes and useful tips on preparing in advance, cooking and serving, this Christmas book will make an invaluable companion for every cook at their busiest time of year.

STARTERS

SMOKED SALMON
WITH DILL PANCAKES

SERVES 4

125 g (4 oz) self raising flour
pinch of salt
½ teaspoon caster sugar
1 egg
1 tablespoon olive oil
150 ml (¼ pint) milk
1 teaspoon wholegrain mustard
2 tablespoons chopped fresh dill
vegetable oil, for frying
250 g (8 oz) smoked salmon
4 tablespoons soured cream
paprika, lime wedges and dill sprigs, to garnish

★

1 Sift flour and salt into a bowl. Stir in sugar.
2 Beat egg and mix with the olive oil, milk, mustard and dill. Pour into flour and whisk, gradually incorporating the flour to make a smooth batter. Transfer to a jug.
3 Heat a little oil in a large frying pan. Pour in a little batter mixture to make a pancake about 6 cm (2½ in) in diameter. Make several more.
4 Cook for 1–2 minutes until golden. Turn over and cook for a further 1–2 minutes. Keep warm while cooking remaining batter.
5 Arrange smoked salmon on 1 large or 4 individual plates. Add a spoonful of soured cream to each pancake and sprinkle with paprika. Serve garnished with lime wedges and dill sprigs.

MUSHROOM SALAD
WITH GARLIC CRUMBS

SERVES 6

1 small raddichio or red chicory
½ an iceberg lettuce
handful of chopped flat-leaved parsley
8 tablespoons olive oil
salt and pepper
250 g (8 oz) button mushrooms
250 g (8 oz) oyster mushrooms
250 g (8 oz) shitake mushrooms
4 rashers of streaky bacon
60 g (2 oz) day old bread
3 garlic cloves, thinly sliced
grated rind of 1 lemon

★

1 Break salad leaves into small pieces and put in a bowl. Add parsley, 2 tablespoons of the oil, salt and pepper and toss well together. Spoon on to plates.
2 Cut any large mushrooms in half. Remove rind from bacon and finely chop the flesh. Crumble bread into small pieces.
3 Heat another 2 tablespoons of the oil in a large frying pan. Add bacon, bread and garlic and fry for about 5 minutes, stirring, until golden. Remove from pan.
4 Add remaining oil to pan with the mushrooms and lemon rind and fry for 3 minutes, stirring.
5 Spoon mushrooms over salad and sprinkle with bacon mixture.

HAM AND ASPARAGUS GRATINS

SERVES 4

12 large asparagus spears
6 slices roast ham
30 g (1 oz) fresh white breadcrumbs
30 g (1 oz) flaked almonds

SAUCE

90 g (3 oz) gruyère or mature Cheddar cheese
45 g ($1\frac{1}{2}$ oz) butter
45 g ($1\frac{1}{2}$ oz) plain flour
470 ml (15fl oz) milk
2 teaspoons French mustard
salt and pepper

1 For sauce, grate the cheese. Melt butter in a small saucepan over a low heat. Add flour and cook for 1 minute, stirring constantly. Remove pan from heat and gradually stir in milk. Return to heat and cook to give a smooth sauce, stirring. Stir in cheese and mustard and season with salt and pepper. Remove pan from heat.
2 Break off and discard woody ends of asparagus spears. Thinly peel stems using a potato peeler. Cook asparagus in a pan of boiling water for 4 minutes, or until tender, then drain.
3 Preheat oven to 190C (375F/ Gas 5). When asparagus spears are cool enough to handle, cut ham slices in half and wrap each piece around an asparagus stem. Arrange ham and asparagus rolls in a lightly greased baking dish. Spoon over sauce and top with breadcrumbs and almonds. Bake in the oven for about 20 minutes until sauce is hot and bubbling and topping is crisp and golden. Serve immediately.

CRISPY BACON AND AVOCADO SALAD

SERVES 4

1 avocado
60 g (2 oz) hazelnuts
6 rashers of streaky bacon
250 g (8 oz) mixed salad leaves

DRESSING

3 tablespoons hazelnut oil
1 tablespoon cider vinegar
1 teaspoon French mustard
1 clove garlic, crushed
salt and pepper

1 For dressing, put all the ingredients in a screw-topped jar and shake to combine.
2 Halve, stone, peel and slice avocado. Pour over dressing.
3 Toast hazelnuts under a grill, stirring until golden. Finely chop.
4 Remove rind from bacon and finely chop the flesh. Dry-fry until crisp, then add to bowl with salad leaves and hazelnuts. Stir until mixed. Serve immediately.

CRUDITIES WITH GARLIC DIP

SERVES 4–6

2 red or yellow peppers
12 radishes
12 baby carrots
$\frac{1}{2}$ a cucumber
125 g (4 oz) small mange-tout
12 baby corn
2 sticks of celery
12 quail's eggs
herb sprigs, to garnish

GARLIC DIP

8 tablespoons mayonnaise
2–3 cloves garlic, crushed
salt and pepper

1 Prepare dip. Mix mayonnaise with garlic and salt and pepper in a bowl.
2 Cut the peppers in half, discard cores and seeds and slice the flesh. Trim the radishes, leaving on a little greenery at the ends. Peel and trim the carrots. Halve the cucumber lengthwise, scoop out the seeds and cut the flesh into sticks. Blanch mange-tout and baby corn in boiling water for 1 minute: refresh in cold water and drain. Trim celery and cut into sticks.
3 Place the quail's eggs in a saucepan of cold water to cover and bring to the boil. Boil for 2 minutes, then plunge the eggs into cold water to cool. Partially peel the eggs.
4 Arrange the vegetables and eggs on a large platter or individual serving plates. Cover and chill until required. Garnish with herb sprigs and serve with garlic dip.

SMOKED SALMON PARCELS

SERVES 4

2 hard-boiled eggs
125 g (4 oz) cream cheese
3 tablespoons double cream
2 teaspoons snipped chives
salt and pepper
4 slices smoked salmon
few whole chives
125 g (4 oz) mixed salad leaves
toast, to serve

DRESSING

4 tablespoons olive oil
2 tablespoons lemon juice
$\frac{1}{2}$ teaspoon French mustard
pinch of sugar

1 Finely chop the eggs and mix with the cream cheese, cream and chives in a bowl. Season with salt and pepper.
2 Lay the smoked salmon slices

flat and divide cream cheese mixture equally between them. Roll or fold the smoked salmon slices to enclose the filling. Secure each parcel by tying together with whole chives and chill in the refrigerator, covered with plastic wrap, until ready to serve.

3 For dressing, put all the ingredients in a screw-topped jar and shake to combine. Season with salt and pepper.

4 Just before serving, put the salad leaves into a bowl, add dressing and toss together gently to combine. Arrange salad leaves on individual plates with the salmon parcels. Serve with toast.

Above: *Smoked Salmon Parcels*

CHESTNUT AND CRANBERRY SAUCE

SERVES 6

1 onion
2 sticks celery
1 tablespoon vegetable oil
940 ml (1½ pints) vegetable stock
bouquet garni
salt and pepper
500 g (1 lb) peeled cooked chestnuts, or one can unsweetened chestnut purée
60 g (2 oz) cranberries
60 ml (2fl oz) port
parsley sprigs and a few whole cranberries, to garnish

1 Chop onion and celery. Heat oil in a saucepan and sauté onion until softened. Add celery, stock, bouquet garni and salt and pepper. Bring to the boil, cover and simmer for 15 minutes.

2 Add chestnuts and cranberries to pan and simmer for 15 minutes. Discard bouquet garni. Allow soup to cool slightly, then blend in a food processor until smooth.

3 Return soup to pan, add port, adjust seasoning and serve garnished with parsley and cranberries.

COOK'S TIP

Fresh cranberries are becoming more widely available at Christmas time. Look out for them at larger supermarkets, or order them through your local greengrocer.

MUSHROOM FILO TARTLETS

SERVES 4

125 g (4 oz) butter
2–3 sheets of filo pastry
2 shallots
375 g (12 oz) mixed mushrooms
1 clove garlic, crushed
4 tablespoons white wine
salt and pepper
herb sprigs, to garnish

1 Preheat oven to 200C (400F/ Gas 6). Melt the butter. Cut filo pastry into twelve 10 cm (4 in) squares and brush liberally with melted butter.
2 Lay a filo square in each of four individual 7.5 cm (3 in) flan tins. Cover each of these with another filo square, moving tins a quarter-turn round. Repeat with remaining squares. Bake in oven for 8–10 minutes until golden. Keep warm.
3 Finely chop shallots. Wipe and chop mushrooms. Heat remaining butter in a frying pan, add garlic and shallots and sauté gently for 5 minutes until just turning golden. Add mushrooms and wine. Cook over a high heat for 2 minutes. Add salt and pepper.
4 Spoon filling into filo cases and garnish with herb sprigs. Serve immediately.

COOK'S TIP

To clarify butter, cut into cubes and melt slowly in a heavy saucepan over a low heat; do not allow to boil. Carefully spoon off the clear butter, leaving the milky sediment behind. Store clarified butter in refrigerator for up to 2 weeks.

ROQUEFORT AND ALMOND SOUP

SERVES 6

1 tablespoon sunflower oil
1 clove garlic
1 tablespoon plain flour
625 ml (1 pint) milk
60 g (2 oz) ground almonds
60 g (2 oz) Roquefort cheese
2 tablespoons chopped chervil or parsley
salt and pepper
chervil or parsley sprigs, and croûtons, to serve

1 Heat oil in a saucepan, add garlic and sauté for 1 minute. Remove from heat and stir in flour, then 155 ml (5fl oz) milk.
2 Add ground almonds to pan then add remaining milk. Return to heat and bring to the boil. Cook for 3 minutes until thickened.
3 Crumble in Roquefort, add herbs and cook gently until cheese has melted. Season. Serve with herbs and croûtons.

CAULIFLOWER AND CRESS SOUP

SERVES 6

1 bunch watercress
1 onion
1 small cauliflower
2 tablespoons vegetable oil
785 ml ($1\frac{1}{4}$ pints) well-flavoured chicken stock
salt and pepper
4 tablespoons single cream
crusty bread, to serve

1 Roughly chop watercress, onion and cauliflower. Heat oil in saucepan, add onion and watercress, cover and cook gently for about 10 minutes until softened.
2 Add cauliflower, stock and salt and pepper. Bring to the boil, cover and simmer for 20 minutes.
3 Cool slightly, then blend in food processor until smooth. Return to pan and heat through. Pour into bowls and add cream. Serve with crusty bread.

MELON AND PARMA HAM

SERVES 4–6

1 small Chanterais melon
1 small Galia or Ogen melon
12 very thin slices Parma ham

DRESSING

60 g (2 oz) dolcelatte cheese
juice of $\frac{1}{2}$ lemon
1–2 teaspoons olive oil
1–2 teaspoons cream or milk
pepper
mint sprigs, to garnish

1 Cut melons into wedges and arrange on serving plates with Parma ham. Cover and chill.
2 For dressing, mash dolcelatte and lemon juice to a paste, then stir in olive oil, cream or milk and pepper.
3 Spoon cheese dressing over melon and garnish with mint.

CHICKEN LIVER MOUSSE

SERVES 4

375 g (12 oz) chicken livers
salt and pepper
1 tablespoon Marsala or brandy
1 tablespoon olive oil
250 g (8 oz) butter
125 ml (4fl oz) double cream
125 ml (4fl oz) clarified butter, see Cook's Tip
4 sage sprigs

1 Cut out and discard any bitter 'green' bits and any fatty 'strings' from livers. Rinse under cold water and pat dry with absorbent kitchen paper.
2 Sprinkle livers liberally with salt and pepper. Place in a shallow dish. Sprinkle with Marsala or brandy and olive oil. Cover and marinate for between 1 and 2 hours, if time permits.
3 Place a non-stick frying pan over a low heat and add livers with marinade. Cook gently, stirring constantly, for 10–12 minutes or until livers are firm but still pink in the middle when pierced with a sharp knife; the livers should not brown. Cool slightly.
4 Beat butter in bowl until softened. Place livers in a food processor and blend, gradually adding butter and working until smooth and creamy. Add cream and blend for 3 seconds. Adjust seasoning.
5 Spoon mousse into four individual ramekin dishes, smooth surface and cover each with a thin layer of clarified butter and a couple of sage leaves, to decorate. Allow to set. Serve with salad leaves and melba toast.

Clockwise from top: *Chicken Liver Mousse; Mushroom Filo Tartlets; and Melon & Parma Ham*

WATERCRESS AND BLUE BRIE SOUP

SERVES 6

2 onions
1 large potato
2 tablespoons vegetable oil
600 ml (1 pint) vegetable stock
150 g (5 oz) watercress
250 g (8 oz) blue brie cheese
salt and pepper
150 ml (5fl oz) double cream
watercress to garnish, if desired

1 Roughly chop onions and cut potato into chunks. Heat oil in a large saucepan. Add onions and fry gently for 5 minutes. Stir in potato, stock and 600 ml (1 pint) water. Bring to the boil. Cover and simmer gently for 10 minutes.

2 Add watercress and cook for 3 minutes then remove from the heat. Cut 6 very thin slices from the firm end of the cheese and reserve for garnish. Roughly chop remaining cheese and add to soup. Blend in a food processor until smooth.

3 Return to saucepan and season lightly with salt and pepper. Pour in half the cream.

4 Ladle into soup bowls and swirl in the remaining cream. Garnish with the reserved cheese, chopped and watercress sprigs, if desired.

SEAFOOD RILLETTES

SERVES 4–6

1 spring onion
180 g (6 oz) peeled prawns
150 g (5 oz) smoked trout
1 tablespoon chopped fresh tarragon
pepper
125 g (4 oz) butter
tarragon sprigs, to garnish
soda bread or oatcakes, to serve

1 Roughly chop spring onion, put in a food processor with prawns and blend until finely chopped.

Turn into a bowl. (Alternatively, finely chop onion and prawns by hand, put in a bowl and mash together).

2 Flake the trout with a fork and add to prawn mixture with the tarragon and pepper.

3 Melt butter and stir about half into the fish mixture. Lightly pack into a 600 ml (1 pint) pâté or soufflé dish. Cover with remaining butter and chill for several hours.

4 Spoon scoops on to serving plates and garnish with tarragon sprigs. Serve with toasted soda bread or oatcakes.

COOK'S TIP

Fresh salmon can be used in place of the smoked trout.

MELON AND PAWPAW SALAD

SERVES 6

1 small charentais melon
½ small Ogen or honeydew melon
2 pawpaws
2 figs
1 piece of stem ginger, plus 4 teaspoons of the syrup
grated rind and juice of 1 lime
6 tablespoons fresh orange juice
mint leaves, to garnish

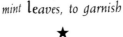

1 Cut the melons in half and remove the seeds with a teaspoon. Scoop out the flesh from both the melons using a melon baller.

2 Halve the pawpaw and remove the seeds. Cut away skin and thinly slice the flesh. Cut each fig into 6 wedges.

3 Put the prepared melons, pawpaws and figs in a bowl. Very thinly slice the stem ginger and add to the bowl.

4 Mix together lime rind and juice, ginger syrup and orange juice and pour over salad. Toss together lightly.

5 Spoon into serving dishes and garnish with mint leaves.

COOK'S TIP

As you are scooping out the melon balls, save any juice and add it to the salad.

THE MAIN EVENT

TRADITIONAL ROAST TURKEY

SERVES 8

5.5 kg (12 lb) oven-ready turkey, thoroughly thawed if frozen
1 onion
2 carrots
2 bay leaves
1 quantity stuffing, see page 20 or below
180 g (6 oz) butter
salt and pepper
bacon kebabs, see page 20
fresh herbs, to garnish

1 Remove giblets from the turkey as soon as possible. Put in a pan with the onion, carrots, bay leaves and 600 ml (1 pint) water. Bring to the boil then simmer for about 1 hour. Strain, cool and reserve.

2 Preheat oven to 190C (375F/ Gas 5). Spoon some stuffing into neck end of the turkey. Form remaining stuffing into small balls. Tuck skin under bird and truss it with the wings folded under the body and the legs tied together. Soften butter and spread over the breast. Season with salt and pepper.

3 Line a large roasting tin with strong, wide foil. Place turkey in tin. Cover with foil, tucking under rim. Cook for $3\frac{1}{4}$ hours.

4 Uncover the turkey. If room, tuck the bacon kebabs and stuffing balls around the turkey. If not, cook in a separate dish. Cook for a further 30 minutes until brown.

5 Test to see if the turkey is cooked, see page 14. Lift turkey from roasting tin, tipping slightly to allow juices to run out. Place on a large warmed serving dish and cover with foil. Leave to stand for up to 30 minutes while preparing gravy, see next recipe.

6 Garnish turkey with bacon kebabs, stuffing balls and herbs.

CHESTNUT, LEEK AND SAGE STUFFING

Enough to stuff a 5.5 kg (12 lb) turkey and make plenty of stuffing balls.

two 425 g (13 oz) cans peeled whole chestnuts
3 leeks
60 g (2 oz) butter
5 tablespoons chopped fresh sage or 4 teaspoons dried
grated rind of 1 lemon
125 g (4 oz) fresh breadcrumbs
salt and pepper
1 egg

1 Finely chop chestnuts in a food processor. (Alternatively, finely chop by hand).

2 Finely chop leeks. Melt butter in a large pan. Add leeks and fry for 3 minutes, stirring. Add the chestnuts, sage, lemon rind, breadcrumbs, salt and pepper.

3 Beat egg, add and mix until thoroughly combined. Cover and chill until ready to use.

BREAD SAUCE

SERVES 8

1 onion
8 whole cloves
900 ml ($1\frac{1}{2}$ pints) milk
3 bay leaves
180 g (6 oz) fresh breadcrumbs
60 g (2 oz) butter
salt and pepper
3 tablespoons double cream

1 Skin onion and stud with the cloves. Put in a saucepan with the milk and bay leaves. Bring just to the boil, then remove from heat and leave for 30 minutes.

2 Remove bay leaves and onion. Stir in breadcrumbs and return to the heat. Simmer gently for 4–5 minutes, until the sauce thickens. Stir in butter, salt and pepper.

3 Just before serving, reheat gently and stir in the cream.

PERFECT GRAVY

SERVES 8

pan juices from cooked turkey
2 tablespoons plain flour
600 ml (1 pint) giblet stock, see previous recipe, step 1
150 ml ($\frac{1}{4}$ pint) red wine
salt and pepper

1 Pour turkey cooking juices from foil into roasting tin. Drain off all but about 1 tablespoon of the fat layer, leaving juices.

2 Add flour and cook, stirring, for 2 minutes. Whisk in stock then red wine.

3 Bring to the boil and simmer gently for 3–4 minutes, until slightly thickened and smooth. Season with salt and pepper.

THAWING

Frozen turkeys must be completely thawed before cooking. Leave in the bag, opened, place on a large plate or tray to catch juices and thaw at room temperature for the time stated in the chart on page 15. Remove giblets as soon as they can be released and use for making stock. To see if bird is thawed, check there are no ice crystals inside the body cavity. The legs should feel flexible, rather than rigid. Rinse the turkey, cover loosely and store in the refrigerator. Once thawed, the turkey should be cooked as soon as possible.

STUFFING

Only stuff the neck cavity of the turkey, being careful not to pack it too tightly. Fold over the neck skin then truss the turkey with the wings folded under the body and the legs tied together. Any excess stuffing can be rolled into small balls and roasted around the turkey for the last 25–30 minutes of cooking time. Alternatively, put it into a separate dish and cook for 1 hour.

If liked, put 2–3 onions and a handful of herbs into the body cavity to give extra flavour.

COOKING

Once stuffed, weigh turkey and calculate cooking time, see the chart on page 15. (Remember that you'll need to allow 30 minutes for the bird to rest before carving and serving, see opposite). Cover the breast with softened butter, then season with salt and pepper.

Line roasting tin with foil, bringing edges up around rim. Place turkey on the foil then cover with another sheet of foil, tucking the edges under the rim. Roasting the turkey in a tent of foil helps keep the meat moist and prevents over-browning. Roast at 190C (375F/Gas 5) for calculated cooking time. Fold back the foil about 30 minutes before end of cooking time to brown skin.

TESTING

To test if turkey is cooked, insert a skewer into the thickest part of the thigh. If juices run clear it is ready, if not, return to the oven for a little longer.

RESTING

Transfer turkey to a large warmed serving dish, cover with foil and leave to rest for about 30 minutes. This allows the flesh to firm up, making carving easier.

LEFTOVERS

Once carved, leave turkey until cold, then cover with foil and refrigerate for up to 2 days. Serve reheated leftovers piping hot.

If freezing leftovers, slice the meat from the bones and freeze in small quantities. Alternatively, cover with stock, gravy, tomato or white sauce. Reheat thoroughly and do not refreeze.

MAKING STOCK

The turkey carcass and bones can be made into a delicious stock for flavouring soups and stews.

Put the bones in a large saucepan. Add 2 roughly chopped onions, carrots and celery sticks, a bouquet garni, bay leaves or thyme. Cover with cold water and bring to the boil. Reduce heat and simmer for about $1\frac{1}{2}$ hours. Cool, strain and refrigerate for up to 2 days or freeze.

CARVING

Turkey is easy to carve provided you have a large, sharp knife and fork to hold the bird steady. Loosen legs from the body so that the breast can be reached easily. On large turkeys the leg meat can be sliced from the bone.

★ TURKEY TIMETABLE ★

Oven-ready weight	Thawing at room temp.	Cooking time at 190C (375F/Gas 5)	Servings (allowing for cold next day)
up to 2.5 kg (5 lb)	10–15 hours	$1\frac{1}{2}$–2 hours	3
2.5–3 kg (5-6 lb)	15–16 hours	2–$2\frac{1}{2}$ hours	4
3–3.1 kg (6–7 lb)	16–17 hours	$2\frac{1}{2}$–3 hours	5
3.1–3.6 kg (7–8 lb)	17–18 hours	3–$3\frac{1}{4}$ hours	6
3.6–5 kg (8–10 lb)	18–22 hours	$3\frac{1}{4}$–$3\frac{3}{4}$ hours	7
5–6 kg (10–12 lb)	22–25 hours	$3\frac{3}{4}$–4 hours	8
6–6.8 kg (12–15 lb)	25–30 hours	4–$4\frac{1}{4}$ hours	8–10
6.8–8.2 kg (15–18 lb)	30–35 hours	$4\frac{1}{4}$–$4\frac{1}{2}$ hours	10–15
8.2–10 kg (18–22 lb)	35–40 hours	$4\frac{1}{2}$–5 hours	15–20

CHRISTMAS COUNTDOWN

Six to eight weeks ahead Make Traditional Christmas Pudding. *One week before Christmas* Calculate thawing time of turkey if using frozen. Make Light Christmas Pudding (if using) and mince pies. *23rd December* Make chosen sauces to accompany turkey and Christmas pudding.

Christmas Eve Make starter from page 6 or 7, if chosen. Prepare batter if using starter on page 4. Make stuffing, Bacon Kebabs and giblet stock for gravy. Prepare vegetables, and refrigerate in polythene bags. Peel potatoes and cover with cold water. Lay table. Chill white wine.

Christmas Day Preparation and cooking times are for a 6 kg (12 lb) turkey. Adjust timetable for a smaller or larger bird. The following times plan for lunch at 2.00pm (or dinner at 8.00pm).

9.15am (3.15pm) Preheat oven to 190C (375F/Gas 5). Stuff turkey and prepare for cooking.

9.45am (3.45pm) Put turkey in oven. Drain and blanch potatoes, ready for roasting.

11.30am (5.30pm) Cook the pudding.

12.15pm (6.15pm) Put potatoes in oven to roast. Put any cold sauces, butters and cream into serving containers. Put mince pies on baking sheet ready to reheat.

12.45pm (6.45pm) Unwrap turkey. Cook Bacon Kebabs and stuffing. Warm plates and serving dishes. Open red wine.

1.15pm (7.15pm) Prepare and take cold starter to table.

1.30pm (7.30pm) Test turkey and keep covered with foil. Make gravy and cook vegetables. Reheat bread sauce and soup, if serving. Cook starters on pages 4–9, if using.

2.00pm (8.00pm) Serve starter. Turn off pudding. Keep vegetables warm. Reheat mince pies.

ROAST POTATOES
WITH GARLIC AND ROSEMARY

SERVES 8

1.5 kg (3 lb) small baking potatoes
salt
3 garlic cloves
6 rosemary sprigs
6 tablespoons olive oil
coarse sea salt, to sprinkle
rosemary sprigs, to garnish

1 Preheat oven to 190C (375F/ Gas 5). Peel and halve potatoes and put in a saucepan. Cover with water, add salt and bring to the boil. Reduce heat and simmer for 2 minutes. Drain well.

2 Slice garlic as thinly as possible. Remove rosemary leaves from stalks and finely chop.

3 Make deep cuts in the potatoes, 5 mm ($\frac{1}{4}$in) apart. Tuck garlic slices into some of the cuts.

4 Place potatoes in a roasting tin and sprinkle with the chopped rosemary and oil. Bake in the oven for about $1\frac{1}{4}$ hours, turning occasionally, until crisp and golden brown.

5 Transfer to a warmed serving dish, sprinkle with coarse salt and garnish with rosemary sprigs.

COOK'S TIP

The potatoes are roasted at a lower temperature than usual as they are being cooked at the same time as the turkey. If roasting at a higher temperature, reduce the cooking time.

SAUTEED LEEKS AND CARROTS

SERVES 8

750 g ($1\frac{1}{2}$ lb) carrots
750 g ($1\frac{1}{2}$ lb) small leeks
salt and pepper
4 tablespoons olive oil
2 tablespoons sesame seeds

1 Peel carrots and cut diagonally into 5 mm ($\frac{1}{4}$ in) slices. Trim leeks and cut diagonally into 1 cm ($\frac{1}{2}$in) slices.

2 Cook carrots in boiling salted water for 2 minutes. Add leeks and cook for a further 1 minute. Drain the vegetables thoroughly.

3 Heat oil in a large frying pan. Add carrots and leeks and cook, stirring frequently, for 4–5

minutes until beginning to colour. Season with salt and pepper.
4 Transfer to a warmed serving dish and sprinkle with the sesame seeds.

BRUSSELS SPROUTS
WITH HAZELNUT BUTTER

SERVES 8

1.25 kg (2½ lb) Brussels sprouts
60 g (2 oz) blanched hazelnuts
60 g (2 oz) butter
salt and pepper
shredded rind of 1 lemon

1 Trim Brussels sprouts and pull off any damaged or discoloured outer leaves. With a sharp knife, make a cross in the stalk end of each one.
2 Toast hazelnuts under a grill for a few minutes, stirring frequently, until golden then finely chop.
3 Melt butter in a saucepan and mix with hazelnuts.
4 Cook Brussels sprouts in boiling salted water for about 8 minutes, until just tender. Drain and return to pan.
5 Add hazelnut butter, lemon rind and a little salt and pepper. Toss ingredients lightly together and transfer to a warmed serving dish.

COOK'S TIP

Although time consuming, it is important to make a cross in the stalks of the Brussels sprouts as it allows the thick part to cook as quickly as the leaves.

CRANBERRY SAUCE

SERVES 8

250 g (8 oz) fresh or frozen cranberries
90 g (3 oz) light muscovado sugar

1 Put cranberries, sugar and 150 ml ($\frac{1}{4}$ pint) water in a pan. Simmer for 10 minutes, until soft.
2 Leave to cool, then transfer to a small dish. Cover and chill.

COOK'S TIPS

If liked, spice up the sauce with $\frac{1}{2}$ teaspoon cinnamon or finely chopped fresh root ginger. The grated rind of an orange or lemon, or a splash of port also tastes good.

ROAST CHICKEN WITH GINGER

SERVES 4

8 small onions
45 g ($1\frac{1}{2}$oz) fresh root ginger
4 spring onions
2–3 sprigs of fresh thyme
4 garlic cloves
250 g (8 oz) mascarpone cheese
salt and pepper
30 g (1 oz) butter
$\frac{1}{2}$teaspoon cornflour
150 ml ($\frac{1}{4}$pint) ginger wine
fresh herbs, to garnish

1 Preheat oven to 180C (350F/ Gas 4). Cut off root ends from onions so they sit flat. Leave unpeeled but pull away any loose layers. Cook in boiling water for 3 minutes then drain.
2 Peel and grate ginger. Trim and finely chop spring onions. Pull leaves from thyme stalks. (You'll need 4–5 teaspoons). Crush the garlic. Mix the ginger, spring onions, thyme and garlic with half of the mascarpone cheese and a little salt and pepper.
3 Tuck your fingers between skin and flesh of chicken to loosen skin over breast and thighs. Using a teaspoon push cheese mixture between skin and flesh. Press down stuffing until evenly distributed.
4 Place chicken and onions in a large roasting tin. Soften butter and dot on onions. Roast for $1\frac{1}{2}$ hours until chicken and onions are golden. Baste chicken after 45 minutes cooking time and cover with foil if sufficiently browned. To test if chicken is cooked, pierce thickest part of thigh with a skewer, the juices should run clear.
5 Transfer chicken and onions to a warmed serving dish and keep warm. Skim off the fat left in roasting tin. Stir cornflour into juices left in pan. Blend in ginger wine, remaining mascarpone cheese, and 75 ml (3fl oz) water. Bring to the boil, stirring until thickened. Garnish chicken with thyme and serve with the gravy.

COOK'S TIPS

For extra flavour, tuck an onion and a bunch of thyme inside chicken before cooking. If chicken has giblets use to make stock and use instead of the water in the gravy.

CUCUMBER SAUTE

SERVES 4

1 large cucumber
2 tablespoons capers
30 g (1 oz) dill cucumbers or gherkins
2 tomatoes
30 g (1 oz) butter
1 tablespoon olive oil
salt and pepper

1 Peel cucumber and halve lengthways. Scoop out soft centres then cut widthways into 1 cm ($\frac{1}{2}$ in) slices.
2 Finely chop capers. Thinly slice dill cucumbers or gherkins. Put tomatoes in a bowl, cover with boiling water for about 40 seconds then plunge into cold water. Peel off the skins. Halve, scoop out seeds and dice the flesh.
3 Melt butter with the oil in a frying pan. Add cucumber and fry for 2–3 minutes, until just softened.
4 Stir in capers, dill cucumbers or gherkins, diced tomato, salt and pepper. Cook, stirring, for 1 minute. Serve hot.

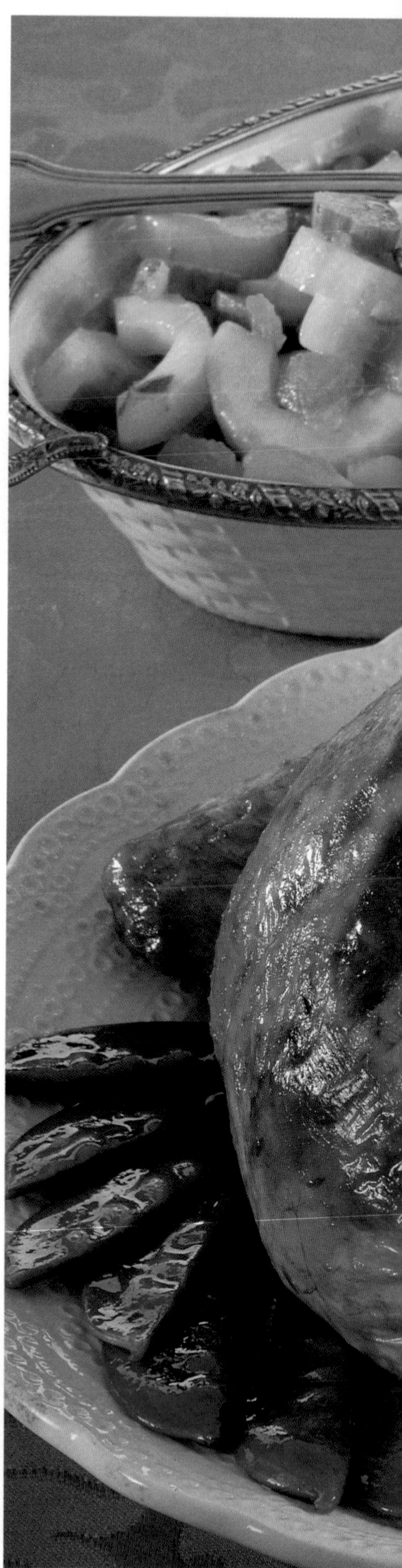

SPICED CHICKEN ROULADE

Chicken breasts, stuffed with spicy apricots and beans, make an ideal meal if just serving two or three people. For a more traditional dish, replace the spicy stuffing with a half quantity of the stuffing on page 12 or the next recipe. Accompany with festive trimmings such as bacon kebabs and cranberry sauce.

SERVES 2–3

2 large chicken breasts
2.5 cm (1 in) piece fresh root ginger
90 g (3 oz) French beans
1 teaspoon coriander seeds
1 teaspoon cumin seeds
90 g (3 oz) no-soak dried apricots
4 no-soak dried prunes
1 onion
1 garlic clove
60 g (2 oz) butter
45 g (1½ oz) fresh breadcrumbs
60 g (2 oz) sausagemeat
1 tablespoon beaten egg
salt and pepper
4 rashers of streaky bacon
150 ml (¼ pint) dry white wine
4 tablespoons double cream
fresh coriander, to garnish

★

1 Preheat oven to 180C (350F/ Gas 4). Using a sharp knife, cut horizontally almost through each chicken breast. Open out, place between two sheets of damp greaseproof paper or cling film then beat with a rolling pin to flatten.
2 Peel and grate ginger. Cook beans in boiling water for 1 minute then drain. Lightly crush coriander and cumin seeds. Chop the apricots and prunes.
3 Finely chop onion and crush garlic. Melt 30 g (1 oz) of the butter in a saucepan. Add onion and garlic and fry for 3 minutes. Stir in ginger, crushed spices, breadcrumbs, sausagemeat, egg, salt and pepper. Beat the ingredients well together until thoroughly combined.
4 Lay a third of the stuffing down centre of one chicken breast. Cover with half the beans and another third of the stuffing. Cover with remaining beans and stuffing. Lay second chicken breast over stuffing and bring up sides to form a roll. Remove rind and any bones from bacon and lay over the chicken.
5 Tie the roll with string, at 2.5 cm (1 in) intervals. Lay the chicken in an ovenproof dish in which it fits snugly. Dot with the remaining 30 g (1 oz) butter and spoon over the white wine.
6 Cover with foil and bake for 30 minutes. Uncover and bake for a further 30 minutes.
7 Leave to stand for 5 minutes then remove string and transfer to a warmed serving dish. Keep warm.
8 Pour the juices from the chicken into a saucepan and stir in cream, salt and pepper. Heat through gently.
9 Slice the roulade and garnish with coriander. Serve with the sauce.

BACON KEBABS

SERVES 8

8 rashers of streaky bacon
8 chipolata sausages
8 apricots
8 prunes

1 Remove the rind and any bones from the bacon rashers. Twist each sausage into three and separate.
2 Thread each rasher on to a wooden skewer, tucking a piece of sausage, apricot, sausage, prune and remaining sausage between the folds of the bacon.
3 Cook with turkey for last 30 minutes of cooking time, or until crisp and golden. Arrange around the turkey to serve.

OATMEAL AND ORANGE STUFFING

Enough to stuff a 5.5 kg (12 lb) turkey and make plenty of stuffing balls.

60 g (2 oz) wild rice
125 g (4 oz) medium oatmeal
500 g (1 lb) onions
60 g (2 oz) butter
grated rind of 2 oranges
90 g (3 oz) raisins
180 g (6 oz) fresh breadcrumbs
salt and pepper
1 egg

1 Cook wild rice in boiling water for 30 minutes, until tender. Drain well.
2 Toast oatmeal under a grill for a few minutes, stirring frequently, until golden. Finely chop the onions. Melt butter in a large saucepan, add onions and fry for 3 minutes.
3 Stir in the rice, oatmeal, orange rind, raisins, breadcrumbs, salt and pepper.
4 Add egg and mix until thoroughly combined. Cover and chill in the refrigerator until ready to use.

ROAST GOOSE
WITH SPICED APPLES AND FIGS

SERVES 8

5–6 kg (10–12 lb) oven-ready goose
1 medium and 1 large onion
1 carrot
1 celery stick
375 g (12 oz) dried figs
60 g (2 oz) butter
180 g (6 oz) fresh breadcrumbs
1 egg
2 tablespoons chopped fresh parsley plus sprigs, to garnish
2 tablespoons chopped fresh thyme plus sprigs, to garnish
salt and pepper
1 small loaf of bread
8 small apples
16 whole cloves
30 g (1 oz) light muscovado sugar
$\frac{1}{2}$ teaspoon ground mixed spice

1 Remove giblets from goose and put in a saucepan, removing liver (see Cook's Tip). Cut the medium onion in half and add to pan with the carrot, celery and 1.1 litre (2 pints) water. Bring to the boil, reduce heat and simmer gently for 1 hour. Strain the giblet stock and reserve.

2 Preheat oven to 180C (350F/Gas 4). Chop the large onion. Chop the figs. Melt 30 g (1 oz) of the butter in a saucepan. Add onion and fry for 3 minutes. Remove from heat and add 250 g (8 oz) of the figs, the breadcrumbs, egg, chopped parsley and thyme. Season lightly with salt and pepper and mix well together.

3 Pack half the stuffing into the neck end of the goose. Tuck flap of skin under bird and truss it with the wings folded under the body and the legs tied together with string. Place goose on a rack standing over a roasting tin. Shape remaining stuffing into 2.5 cm (1 inch) balls.

4 Remove crust from loaf of bread and push bread into body cavity of bird to absorb fat during roasting. Cook goose in the oven for $2\frac{3}{4}$ hours.

5 Meanwhile, core apples and cut a thin slice off top of each. Stud each apple with 2 whole cloves. Stand in a roasting tin. Mix the remaining chopped figs with sugar and mixed spice and pack into apples, letting excess stuffing rest on top of the apples. Melt remaining butter and pour over apples.

6 Thirty minutes before end of goose roasting time, place apples and stuffing balls in oven, basting the apples frequently with butter.

7 To test if goose is cooked, pierce thickest part of thigh with a skewer, the juices should run clear. If not cooked, return to oven for a little longer.

8 Transfer goose to a large, warmed serving dish and surround with the spiced apples and stuffing balls. Keep warm.

9 Pour off all the fat from roasting tin. Add 600 ml (1 pint) reserved giblet stock, making up with water if necessary. Bring to the boil and season lightly with salt and pepper. Strain into a warmed gravy boat or jug.

10 Garnish goose with sprigs of parsley and thyme and serve with the gravy.

COOK'S TIPS

If liked, reserve the goose liver, chop it finely and add to the stuffing, frying it with the onion.

Roast potatoes are delicious cooked in goose fat. Add them to the roasting tin about 1 hour before the end of cooking time.

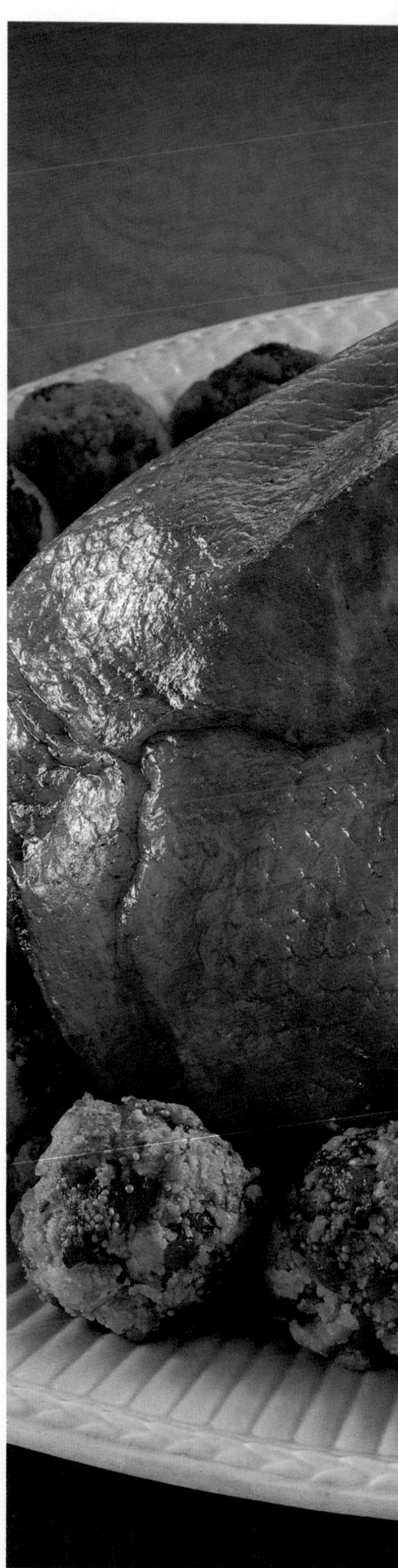

BAKED POTATOES AND PARSNIPS

SERVES 4

750 g ($1\frac{1}{2}$ lb) parsnips
500 g (1 lb) small baking potatoes
salt and pepper
1 small onion
75 ml (3fl oz) hot chicken or vegetable stock
60 g (2 oz) butter
rosemary sprigs, to garnish

1 Preheat oven to 180C (350F/ Gas 4). Peel and thinly slice parsnips and potatoes.
2 Put the potatoes in a saucepan of cold salted water. Bring to the boil and cook for 2 minutes with the lid off. Drain well.
3 Layer half the potatoes and parsnips in an ovenproof dish. Finely slice the onion and add three-quarters to the dish. Cover with remaining potatoes and parsnips.
4 Pour over the hot stock, then sprinkle with remaining onions. Melt the butter, pour over onions and season lightly with salt and pepper.
5 Bake in the oven for $1\frac{1}{4}$–$1\frac{1}{2}$ hours until golden. Garnish with rosemary sprigs.

COOK'S TIP

Don't be tempted to prepare this dish too far in advance as the potatoes and the parsnips tend to discolour if left too long before cooking. Once cooked it will keep well without spoiling.

CREAMY CELERIAC PUREE

SERVES 8

1.5 kg (3 lb) celeriac
30 g (1 oz) butter
1 tablespoon wholegrain mustard
4 tablespoons double cream
salt and pepper
snipped fresh chives, to garnish

1 Peel celeriac and cut into small chunks. Immediately put in a saucepan of water and bring to the boil. Cook for 20 minutes or until softened. Drain well.
2 Mash the celeriac with the butter and mustard until completely smooth.
3 Return to pan and reheat gently. Stir in cream, salt and

pepper. Transfer to a warmed serving dish and garnish with snipped chives.

CREAMY ONION SAUCE

SERVES 8

375 g (12 oz) onions
30 g (1 oz) butter
450 ml ($\frac{3}{4}$ pint) milk
freshly grated nutmeg
60 g (2 oz) fresh breadcrumbs
2 tablespoons chopped fresh parsley
4 tablespoons double cream
salt and pepper

1 Finely chop the onions. Melt butter in a saucepan, add onions and fry gently for 3 minutes.

2 Add the milk, $\frac{1}{4}$ teaspoon grated nutmeg and the breadcrumbs. Bring to the boil, reduce heat and simmer gently for 6–8 minutes, until pulpy.

3 Stir in parsley, cream, salt and pepper and heat through gently. Transfer to a warmed sauceboat or jug and sprinkle with extra grated nutmeg.

COOK'S TIP

This sauce has a very thick consistency that is spooned rather than poured. Although a classic accompaniment to roast goose, it's also good with roast turkey. It can be made in advance and stored in the refrigerator for several days. If necessary, thin down with a little extra cream or milk when reheating.

STIR-FRIED CABBAGE
WITH CRISPY BACON

SERVES 8

1 medium cabbage
4 rashers of streaky bacon
2 tablespoons olive oil
2 tablespoons sunflower seeds
salt and pepper

1 Shred cabbage, discarding central core. Finely dice the bacon.

2 In a large frying pan, fry bacon in its own fat, until turning golden. Add cabbage, oil, sunflower seeds, salt and pepper.

3 Fry for 3–4 minutes, stirring, until crisp. Transfer to a warmed serving dish.

ROAST DUCK
WITH CRANBERRIES AND CLEMENTINES

SERVES 4

2.5 kg (5 lb) oven-ready duckling
½ teaspoon ground allspice
salt and pepper
1 orange
4 clementines
30 g (1 oz) butter
2 cinnamon sticks, halved
180 g (6 oz) fresh or frozen cranberries
5 tablespoons light muscovado sugar
2 teaspoons white wine vinegar
2 tablespoons Cointreau
flat-leaved parsley, to garnish

1 Preheat oven to 220C (425F/Gas 7). Using a fork, pierce duckling all over, except breast area. Rub skin with allspice and sprinkle with salt and pepper. Place duckling on a rack, over a roasting tin. Cook for 15 minutes. Reduce oven temperature to 190C (375F/Gas 5) and cook for a further 1 hour.

2 Pare thick strips of rind from the orange. Squeeze juice and reserve. Peel clementines, leaving them whole. Melt butter in a small saucepan. Add orange rind, cinnamon sticks and whole clementines and cook for 1 minute. Place clementines and orange rice around the duckling and pour over remaining butter. Return to oven for a further 45 minutes.

3 Pour reserved orange juice and the cranberries in the butter pan. Simmer gently for about 10 minutes, until cranberries pop.

4 Transfer duckling, clementines and orange peel to a warmed serving dish and keep warm. Drain off fat from roasting tin, then add cranberries and juice, sugar, vinegar and Cointreau. Bring to the boil, stirring. Season with salt and pepper to taste.

5 Spoon cranberries around duckling and garnish with parsley. Serve with the gravy.

COOK'S TIPS

When serving duckling, carve it in the same way as you would a chicken or turkey, first removing the legs and then taking thin slices from the breast. Although there's not as much flesh on a duckling, the meat is richer so portions needn't be large.

GLAZED TURNIPS WITH BEANS

SERVES 4

750 g (1½ lb) baby turnips
salt and pepper
125 g (4 oz) French beans
30 g (1 oz) butter
2 teaspoons caster sugar
flat-leaved parsley, to garnish

1 Trim ends from turnips and peel. Cut each turnip into 4 or 6 wedges, depending on size. Cook in boiling salted water for about 5 minutes, until almost tender then drain. Cut beans into 5 cm (2 in) lengths and cook in boiling salted water for 2 minutes then drain.

2 Melt the butter in a heavy based frying pan. Add turnips and sprinkle with the sugar.

3 Fry over a moderate heat, stirring, until the turnips begin to colour and turn glossy. Add the beans and heat through for 1–2 minutes.

4 Season lightly with salt and pepper and turn into a warmed serving dish. Serve garnished with flat-leaved parsley.

SWEET POTATO CAKE

SERVES 4

1 kg (2 lb) sweet potatoes
1 ripe pear
60 g (2 oz) butter
3 tablespoons honey
salt and pepper

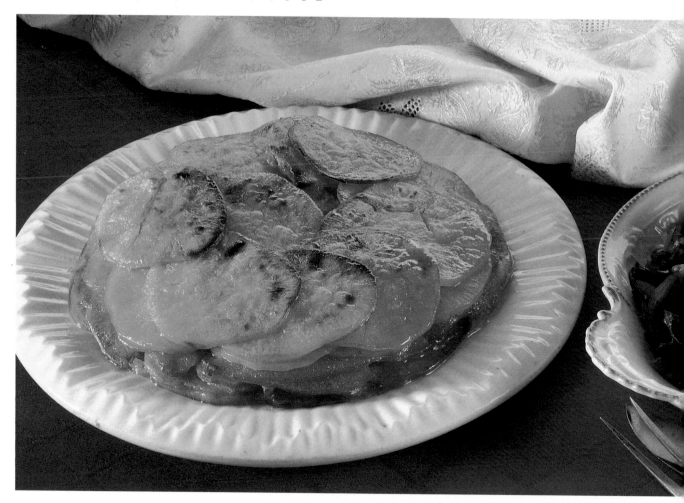

1 Cook the potatoes in their skins, in boiling water for 30–40 minutes, until tender then drain.
2 Preheat oven to 200C (400F/ Gas 6). Grease and base line a 20 cm (8 in) sandwich tin with greaseproof paper.
3 Peel and slice the potatoes as thinly as possible. Peel, core and very thinly slice pear.
4 Pack half the potato slices into tin. Cover with the pear slices, then remaining potato.
5 Melt butter and mix with the honey, salt and pepper. Pour over potatoes. Cover with foil and bake for 45 minutes.
6 Invert on to a flameproof plate and remove paper. Cook under a hot grill for 2–3 minutes, until brown. Serve cut into wedges.

SWEET POTATOES

Sweet potatoes, with their rough, reddish skins and misshapen appearance, are readily available throughout the winter. Boiled just like ordinary potatoes, they have a creamy white flesh that mashes well. Their sweet, earthy taste is delicious in this layered vegetable accompaniment and is perfect with any rich game dish.

ROAST PHEASANT

SERVES 4

2 oven-ready pheasants
6 rashers of smoked streaky bacon
3 onions
2–3 bay leaves
salt and pepper
500 g (1 lb) red cabbage
15 g ($\frac{1}{2}$oz) butter
2 tablespoons olive oil
45 g ($1\frac{1}{2}$oz) pistachio nuts
5 teaspoons redcurrant jelly
$\frac{1}{2}$teaspoons cornflour
5 tablespoons port
150 ml ($\frac{1}{4}$pint) chicken stock
bunches of fresh herbs, to garnish

1 Preheat oven to 200C (400F/ Gas 6). Rinse and dry pheasants and remove any stray feathers. Lay

3 rashers of bacon over each and place in a roasting tin. Halve 1 onion and tuck half inside each bird with the bay leaves. Season lightly with salt and pepper.

2 Roast the pheasants for 1 hour basting frequently during cooking. Meanwhile, shred the cabbage, discarding core. Slice remaining onions.

3 About 20 minutes before pheasants are cooked, melt butter with the olive oil in a saucepan. Add cabbage, onions and pistachio nuts and cook gently for about 8 minutes, stirring frequently, until softened but retaining some texture.

4 Stir 3 teaspoons of the redcurrant jelly into the cabbage and stir until melted. Season lightly with salt and pepper.

5 Transfer pheasants to a warmed serving dish and keep warm. Drain off all but 1 tablespoon of the fat layer, retaining juices. Stir cornflour into juices, then blend in port, remaining 2 teaspoons redcurrant jelly and the stock.

6 Bring to the boil and simmer for 2 minutes, until thickened. Season lightly with salt and pepper and pour into a warmed sauceboat or jug. Garnish pheasant with fresh herbs and serve with the red cabbage and gravy.

COOK'S TIP

Roast pheasants, because like all game birds they lack fat, have a tendency to be dry. To overcome this, always roast them in a jacket of fatty bacon. This will help to maintain their succulence and also crisp and flavour the skin.

PHEASANT

Fresh pheasant makes a perfect choice for a small festive gathering as one pheasant will generously serve two people. Most supermarkets sell oven-ready pheasants, over the Christmas season, which have sufficient flavour for most tastes. If, however, you prefer a more gamey taste, you might prefer to order them from a good butcher or poulterer who sell hung pheasants as these have a stronger flavour. Traditionally, pheasant is served with game chips (thinly sliced and deep fried potatoes) but the Sweet Potato Cake opposite, makes a delicious alternative accompaniment.

GLAZED BAKED HAM

A beautifully presented joint of ham not only makes a delicious addition to a traditional Christmas roast but is also a delicious meal on its own.

SERVES 8

2.5 kg (5 lb) smoked or unsmoked middle gammon
1 onion
whole cloves
1 carrot
1 celery stick
1 bouquet garni
2.5 cm (1 in) piece of fresh root ginger
45 g (1½ oz) light muscovado sugar
25 ml (1fl oz) orange juice
1 tablespoon honey
12 kumquats
bay leaves, to garnish

1 Soak gammon for 12 hours or overnight in a bowl of cold water, then drain.
2 Place gammon in a saucepan. Skin and stud onion with 10 cloves. Add to pan with the carrot, celery and bouquet garni. Cover with cold water and bring to the boil. Reduce heat, cover with a lid and simmer for 1¼ hours. Leave to cool slightly in pan, then drain.
3 Meanwhile, peel and grate the ginger. Mix in a bowl with the sugar, orange juice and honey.
4 Preheat oven to 200C (400F/ Gas 6). Loosen one corner of the gammon skin with a knife. Pull skin away from fat and discard.
5 Using the tip of a sharp knife score wavy lines diagonally across the fat, 2.5 cm (1 in) apart.
6 Thinly slice kumquats. Press a clove through centre of a kumquat slice and press into gammon fat. Continue adding more cloves and kumquat slices to garnish fat, spacing them about 4 cm (1½ in) apart.
7 Line an ovenproof dish or roasting tin with foil. Place gammon in dish and brush all over with some of the glaze. Bake for 30–40 minutes, basting frequently with more glaze, until golden.
8 Transfer to a serving dish. Serve hot or cold, garnished with bay leaves.

COOK'S TIP

I suggest using a middle cut piece of gammon as it looks spectacular and is very easy to carve.

BAKED POTATOES WITH SOURED CREAM

SERVES 8

8 medium baking potatoes
½ teaspoon curry powder
1 tablespoon vegetable oil
30 g (1 oz) butter
300 ml (½ pint) soured cream
2 tablespoons wholegrain mustard
salt and pepper

1 Preheat oven to 200C (400F/ Gas 6). Scrub potatoes and prick all over with a fork. Mix together the curry powder and oil and brush over the potatoes.
2 Bake potatoes in the oven for 1–1¼ hours, until they feel soft when squeezed.
3 Cut each potato in half and lightly fluff up the flesh with a fork. Dot the potato halves with butter.
4 Mix together the soured cream, mustard, salt and pepper. Spoon over the potatoes and serve immediately.

GARLICKY COURGETTES AND CORN

SERVES 8

4 courgettes
250 g (8 oz) baby corn
30 g (1 oz) butter
3 garlic cloves
1 tablespoon vegetable oil
salt and pepper

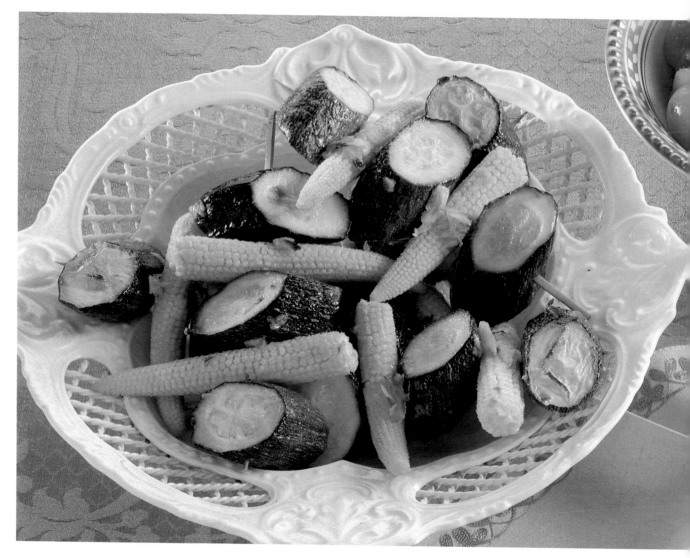

1 Cut courgettes diagonally into chunks. Bring a saucepan of water to the boil. Add corn and cook for 30 seconds. Add courgettes and cook for a further 30 seconds, then drain well.

2 Thread the courgettes and corn on to metal or wooden skewers and arrange on a grill rack.

3 Melt the butter. Crush the garlic, add to the butter with the oil, salt and pepper and mix together. Brush over vegetables.

4 Cook under a moderate grill for about 5 minutes, turning frequently and brushing with more garlic butter, until golden. Serve hot.

COOK'S TIP

If you haven't any skewers, arrange vegetables in a single layer on a foil lined grill rack. Cook as above, turning and brushing frequently with the butter.

SPICED FRUIT COMPOTE

SERVES 8

250 g (8 oz) onions
5 tablespoons white wine vinegar
60 g (2 oz) redcurrant jelly
375 g (12 oz) kumquats
8 ripe plums
4 tablespoons port
4 tablespoons orange juice
1 tablespoon Worcestershire sauce
$\frac{1}{2}$ teaspoon paprika
$\frac{1}{2}$ teaspoon cornflour

1 Slice the onions and put in a pan with vinegar and redcurrant jelly. Cover and cook gently for

10 minutes, until softened.
2 Prick kumquats with a fork, add to pan and cook for 5 minutes, stirring frequently, until kumquats are softened.
3 Meanwhile, cut plums in half and remove stones. Add plums, port, orange juice, Worcestershire sauce and paprika to the kumquats and cook for a further 2 minutes.
4 Blend cornflour with a little water, then add to pan. Bring to the boil, stirring. Turn into a serving dish and serve hot or cold.

COOK'S TIP

This accompaniment has a very chunky texture. For a smoother texture, blend lightly in a food processor and reheat if liked.

SHREDDED CABBAGE
WITH ORANGE AND CARAWAY

SERVES 8

1 small cabbage
30 g (1 oz) butter
2 teaspoons olive oil
1 teaspoon caraway seeds
grated rind of ½ an orange
salt and pepper
shredded orange rind to garnish

1 Roughly shred the cabbage, discarding the stalk. Cook in boiling salted water for 2 minutes then drain thoroughly.
2 Melt the butter in the cleaned saucepan with the olive oil. Add the caraway seeds and grated orange rind and stir.
3 Add the cabbage and cook gently for 1–2 minutes, until heated through. Season lightly with salt and pepper.
4 Transfer to a warmed serving dish and serve garnished with shredded orange rind.

COOK'S TIPS

Use a cabbage with deep green leaves. Fennel, sesame, sunflower or pumpkin seeds can be used too.

BAKED SALMON WITH SPICES

Fish makes an excellent alternative to the traditional meats at Christmas, particularly if you cook it in an interesting way. A whole baked salmon looks particularly impressive and is very easy to prepare. Serve it with the spicy hollandaise sauce and accompaniments on the following pages.

SERVES 4–6

60 g (2 oz) butter
1–1.5 kg (2–3 lb) whole salmon, cleaned
150 ml ($\frac{1}{4}$ pint) white wine
salt
1 teaspoon black peppercorns
2 teaspoons coriander seeds
2 teaspoons mustard seeds
2 teaspoons fennel seeds
sliced limes, fresh coriander and bay leaves, to garnish

1 Preheat oven to 150C (300F/Gas 2). Melt the butter. Spread a double thickness of foil, large enough to wrap the salmon, with some of the melted butter.
2 Lay salmon on foil then loosely bring up sides of foil to make a container. Pour the wine and a little salt over salmon. Secure foil together so that parcel is tightly sealed but leaves space around the salmon. Place on a large baking sheet and cook for 1–1$\frac{1}{4}$hours until tender. To test if salmon is cooked, push a knife into thickest part of flesh near the backbone. The flesh in the centre should have turned opaque. If necessary, re-wrap and cook for a little longer.
3 Meanwhile, grind the peppercorns, coriander, mustard and fennel seeds in a coffee grinder or pestle and mortar until fairly fine.
4 Remove salmon from oven and fold back foil. Raise oven temperature to 200C (400F/Gas 6). Carefully transfer salmon to a chopping board. Using a sharp knife, cut through skin around head and tail, and down back of fish. Carefully peel away skin and any dark brown flesh.
5 Brush pink flesh with melted butter and coat with half the spice mixture.
6 Carefully turn fish over and skin other side. Brush with remaining butter and coat with remaining spice mixture. Turn fish back to original side and place on a clean piece of buttered foil.
7 Bake for a further 5 minutes then transfer to a warmed serving dish. Surround with plenty of sliced limes, coriander and bay leaves and serve hot.

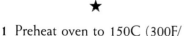

COOK'S TIP

This is the easiest way to cook a small salmon as it requires no specialist equipment, although a fish kettle can be used if you have one. Half fill it with water, adding a little white wine, salt and pepper. Bring to simmering point then lower the salmon, on the rack, into the water. Return to a gentle simmer and cook for 5 minutes per 500 g (1 lb). Leave to drain for 5 minutes then continue from step 4.

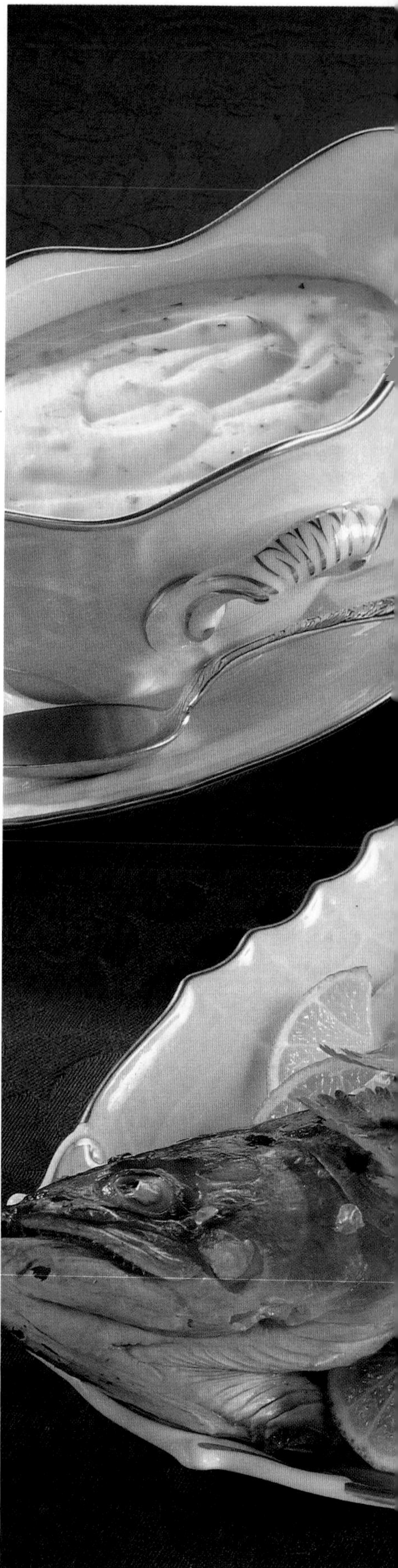

BUTTERED RICE CASTLES

SERVES 6

60 g (2 oz) wild rice
salt and pepper
180 g (6 oz) brown rice
180 g (6 oz) long grain white rice
60 g (2 oz) split red lentils
45 g ($1\frac{1}{2}$ oz) butter

1 Cook wild rice in boiling salted water for 30 minutes until tender then drain. Cook brown rice in boiling salted water for 20–25 minutes until tender then drain.
2 Cook long grain rice and split red lentils together in boiling salted water for 8–10 minutes until just tender then drain.
3 Preheat oven to 200C (400F/ Gas 6). Melt the butter. Brush bases and sides of 6 dariole moulds or individual pudding basins with a little of the butter.
4 Pack long grain rice mixture into bases of moulds. Spoon wild rice into moulds and press down lightly. Spoon brown rice into moulds and pack down lightly. Spoon remaining butter over the rice.
5 Place moulds in a roasting tin and add 1 cm ($\frac{1}{2}$in) depth of boiling water to tin. Cover with foil and cook for 10 minutes.
6 Loosen sides of moulds with a knife then tap rice out on to a serving plate. Keep warm until ready to serve.

HOT MUSHROOM SALAD

SERVES 6

500 g (1 lb) oyster mushrooms
180 g (6 oz) mange-tout
4 tablespoons walnut or olive oil
1 tablespoon balsamic vinegar
salt and pepper
30 g (1 oz) ground almonds

1 Halve any large mushrooms. Trim and halve mange-tout.
2 Heat oil in a frying pan. Add mushrooms and mange-tout and fry for 2 minutes, until just softened.
3 Stir in the vinegar, salt and pepper and turn into a shallow

heatproof serving dish. Sprinkle with the almonds.

4 Cook under a moderate grill until almonds are just beginning to colour. Serve hot.

COOK'S TIP

Try to make use of the various interesting types of mushrooms available at this time of year. If, however, you can only buy ordinary fresh mushrooms, add some dried mushrooms, such as porcini, to liven up the salad. These can now be found in most supermarkets. Soak the dried mushrooms in water, to soften, before use then cook them as above. Oyster mushrooms now come in yellow and pink shades as well as their natural beige.

CORIANDER HOLLANDAISE

SERVES 6

180 g (6 oz) butter
3 tablespoons white wine vinegar
3 egg yolks
$\frac{1}{4}$ teaspoon curry paste
5 tablespoons chopped fresh coriander
few drops of lime or lemon juice
salt and pepper

1 Beat butter until softened. Put vinegar in a small saucepan and boil rapidly until reduced to 1 tablespoon. Put in a large heatproof bowl and add the egg yolks and curry paste.

2 Stand the bowl over a saucepan of hot water. Add a knob of the butter to bowl and whisk well. When melted, gradually add remaining butter, whisking well after each addition, until sauce is thickened.

3 Stir in the coriander, lime or lemon juice, salt and pepper. Transfer to a sauce boat or jug.

COOK'S TIPS

Don't let the water get too hot or the sauce may curdle. If it does, beat in a tablespoon of hot water. If this fails, start again with another egg yolk and gradually beat in the curdled sauce. Once made, Hollandaise sauce will keep, covered, for up to 30 minutes.

CELEBRATION SEAFOOD STEW

A seafood stew, comprising several different types of fish, makes a delicious meal for adventurous diners. Although there's a fair amount of preparation involved, the first nine steps can be done several hours in advance, ready for last minute assembly. Serve with a bowl of steaming baby potatoes and a dish of Rouille (see next recipe).

SERVES 6

500 g (1 lb) red snapper or red mullet
12 tiger prawns
750 g ($1\frac{1}{2}$ lb) cod or haddock fillet
250 g (8 oz) scallops
500 g (1 lb) fresh mussels
1 onion
salt and pepper
1 teaspoon saffron strands
4 tablespoons olive oil
3 tablespoons brandy
2 leeks
4 celery sticks
4 garlic cloves
pared rind of 1 small orange
8 sprigs of fresh thyme
3 bay leaves
300 ml ($\frac{1}{2}$ pint) white wine
1 dressed crab, weighing about 180 g (6 oz)
150 ml ($\frac{1}{4}$ pint) double cream

1 Working on a sheet of newpaper, run a knife from tail to head of snapper or mullet to remove scales. Cut off heads and tails and reserve for making the stock. Make a cut along back of fish then ease the fillet away from the bone using a sharp knife and working with short, sharp strokes. Turn fish over and remove other fillet in same way. Cut fillets into large chunks.

2 Remove heads and shells from prawns leaving tails intact. Reserve trimmings.

3 Skin the cod or haddock and cut flesh into large chunks, discarding any bones. Halve scallops if large.

4 Scrub mussels, discarding any damaged or open shells. Put in a large bowl and, under cold running water, scrape off any sand or mud. Knock off any barnacles with a knife and tug off the beard. Rinse again and discard any that do not close when tapped sharply with a knife.

5 Put all the fish trimmings (except rejected mussels) in a saucepan with the onion, salt, pepper and 1.1 litre (2 pints) water. Bring to the boil, reduce heat and simmer gently for 30 minutes. Cool slightly then strain stock.

6 Put saffron in a bowl, add 1 tablespoon boiling water and leave until needed.

7 Heat 2 tablespoons of the oil in a frying pan. Add snapper or mullet, cod or haddock and scallops and fry, stirring, for 1 minute. Add brandy and light with a taper. When flames die down, remove from heat.

8 Thinly slice leeks, thickly slice celery and crush garlic. Heat remaining oil in a saucepan. Add leeks, celery, garlic, orange rind, thyme and bay leaves and gently fry.

9 Make strained stock up to 1 litre ($1\frac{3}{4}$ pints) with water. Add to vegetables with the wine and saffron. Bring to the boil, cover with a lid and simmer very gently for 15–20 minutes, until vegetables are tender.

10 Add the fried fish and juices, crab and prawns to pan. Stir in cream, salt and pepper and bring almost to the boil. Scatter mussels over stew and cover with lid. Cook for 3–4 minutes, until mussels have opened. Discard any mussels that do not open.

11 Remove half the mussels from their shells and gently stir into the stew. Serve hot with Rouille.

COOK'S TIP

When making this seafood stew, you may need to alter the ingredients depending on the availability of the fish and also personal preference. Halibut and monkfish can be used instead of the cod or haddock, while small cockles can replace the mussels. Cleaned squid, cut into rings, can be used instead of the scallops. Whichever you use, don't forget that fish needs very little cooking. Over-cooking will produce disappointing results.

ROUILLE

SERVES 4–6

1 red pepper
1 red or green chilli
2 garlic cloves
5 tablespoons olive oil
30 g (1 oz) fresh breadcrumbs
salt

1 Cut pepper in half, discard core and seeds, and roughly chop flesh. Cut chilli in half and discard seeds.

2 Put pepper, chilli, garlic and oil in a food processor and blend until smooth. Add breadcrumbs and a little salt and blend to a paste.

3 Transfer to a small serving bowl. Cover and refrigerate until ready to serve.

COOK'S TIP

Warn guests to take rouille cautiously! Usually a half teaspoon is sufficient to spice up a portion of stew.

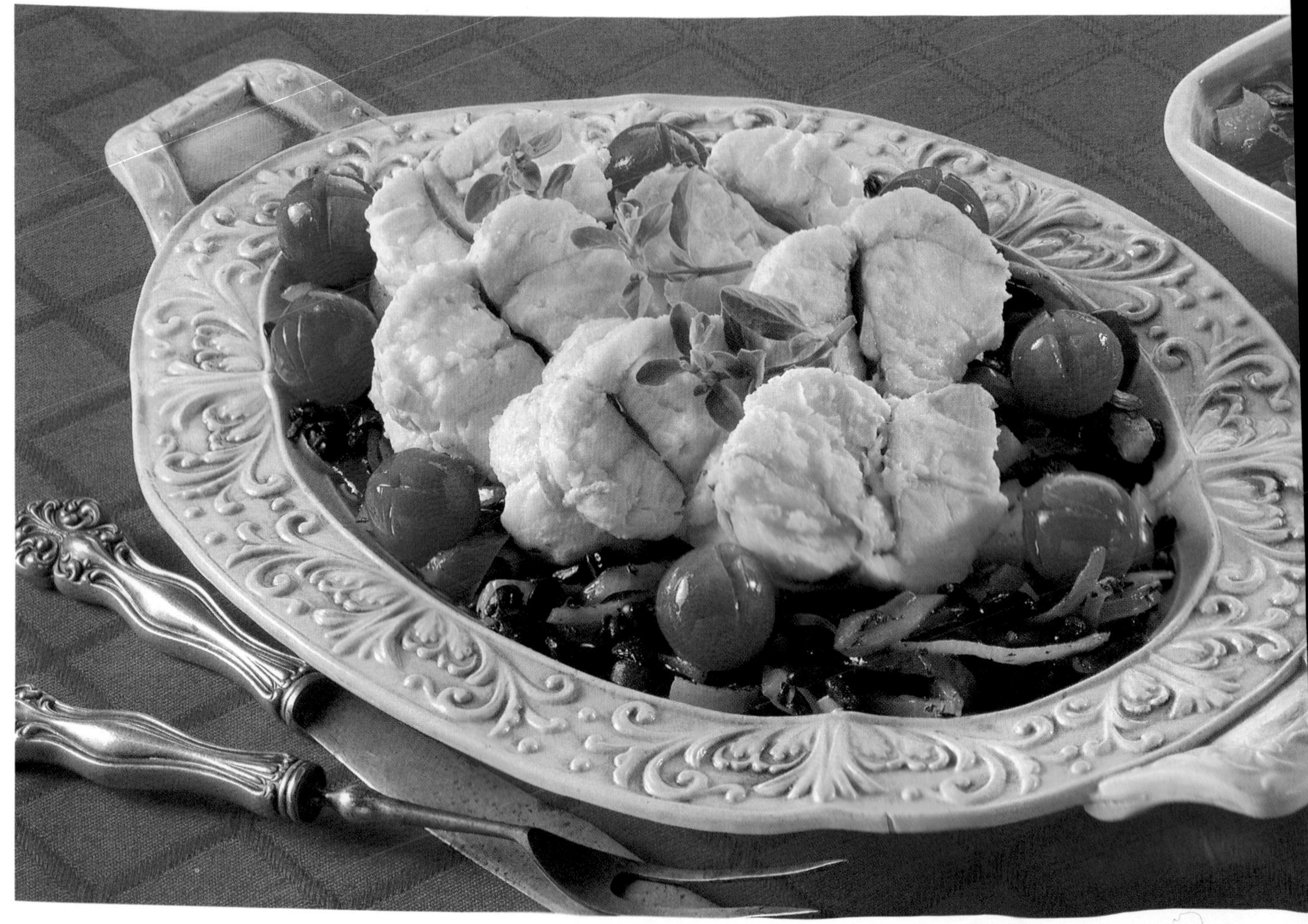

ROASTED MONKFISH
WITH BLACK BEANS

SERVES 4

250 g (8 oz) black beans
1 large monkfish tail, weighing about 1 kg (2 lb)
6 garlic cloves
4 tablespoons olive oil
1 red onion, sliced
2 tablespoons chopped fresh oregano
150 ml ($\frac{1}{4}$ pint) white wine
salt and pepper
125 g (4 oz) red or yellow cherry tomatoes
sprigs of oregano, to garnish

★

1 Wash the beans, put in a large bowl and cover with plenty of cold water. Leave to soak overnight.
2 The next day, drain the beans and put in a large saucepan. Cover with fresh cold water and bring to the boil. Boil rapidly for 10 minutes. Reduce heat and simmer gently for about 30 minutes or until just tender then drain well.
3 Preheat oven to 190C (375F/ Gas 5). Remove any loose skin from monkfish. Cut away central bone to leave 2 long fillets.
4 Lay fillets, side by side, with a thick end against a thin. Using fine string, tie the fillets together at 2.5 cm (1 in) intervals. Slice garlic and tuck half the slices between the fillets.
5 Heat 2 tablespoons of the oil in a frying pan, add the monkfish and fry on all sides, until just turning brown. Drain on absorbent kitchen paper.
6 Slice the onion. Heat remaining oil in pan. Add onion and remaining garlic and fry for 3 minutes, until onion is softened. Stir in beans, oregano, wine, salt and pepper. Bring to the boil then turn into a shallow ovenproof dish.
7 Lay the monkfish on top and season lightly with salt and pepper. Bake in the oven for 10 minutes. Cut a cross in the top of each tomato and add to the dish. Cook for a further 10 minutes or until fish is cooked through. Test by piercing the thick end of a fillet with a sharp knife — the centre should be opaque. If is isn't, cook for a few minutes more.
8 Serve hot, garnished with sprigs of oregano.

HALIBUT PITHIVIERS

SERVES 4–6

750 g (1½ lb) halibut steaks
1 large fennel head
60 g (2 oz) butter
grated rind of 1 lemon
5 tablespoons chopped fresh parsley
salt and pepper
500 g (1 lb) puff pastry
beaten egg, to glaze
1 red pepper
1 yellow pepper
6 stoned black olives
1 tablespoon olive oil
½ teaspoon mild chilli seasoning
400 g (14 oz) can chopped tomatoes
½ teaspoon caster sugar
fresh herbs to garnish

1 Preheat oven to 200C (400F/Gas 6). Using a sharp knife, cut the 4 sections of flesh from each halibut steak, discarding the skin and bones.
2 Trim and thinly slice fennel. Melt 15 g (½ oz) of the butter in a small saucepan. Add fennel and fry gently for 5 minutes, until softened. Remove from the heat and stir in lemon rind, parsley, salt and pepper.
3 Halve the pastry. On a lightly floured surface, roll out one half and cut out a 23 cm (9 in) round. Transfer to a dampened baking sheet. Arrange fish pieces, in a single layer, over pastry round to within 2.5 cm (1 in) of edge. Season with salt and pepper.
4 Spread fennel mixture to within 2.5 cm (1 in) of edges of fish. Dot the fennel with remaining butter.
5 Roll out remaining pastry and cut out a 24 cm (9½ in) round. Brush edges of pastry base with beaten egg then cover with larger circle. Press edges together firmly and flute with the back of a knife. Brush with beaten egg. Using tip of knife, make a decorate pattern from centre to edges. Bake fór 30–35 minutes, until well risen and golden.
6 Meanwhile, cut peppers in half, discard cores and seeds and dice flesh. Quarter olives lengthways. Heat oil in a saucepan. Add peppers, olives, chilli powder, tomatoes and sugar and bring to the boil. Simmer gently for 6–8 minutes, until slightly thickened.
7 Spoon sauce on to warmed serving plates. Cut slices from the pie and place on sauce. Serve garnished with fresh herbs.

FESTIVE VEGETABLE PIE

Packed with chestnuts, stuffing balls and a feast of wintery vegetables, this delicious pie makes a perfect main dish for a special gathering.

SERVES 6–8

STUFFING BALLS

1 large onion
4 garlic cloves
4 tablespoons olive oil
60 g (2 oz) freshly grated Parmesan cheese
250 g (8 oz) fresh breadcrumbs
5 tablespoons chopped fresh herbs
grated rind of 1 orange
salt and pepper
1 egg, beaten

PIE

500 g (1 lb) leeks
500 g (1 lb) turnips
500 g (1 lb) carrots
4 tablespoons olive oil
2 tablespoons plain flour
300 ml (½ pint) white wine
900 ml (1½ pint) vegetable stock
3 bay leaves
1 large parsnip
250 g (8 oz) button mushrooms
250 g (8 oz) can whole chestnuts
750 g (1½ lb) puff pastry
beaten egg, to glaze

1 To make the stuffing balls, finely chop onion and crush garlic. Heat 2 tablespoons of the oil in a saucepan. Add onion and garlic and fry gently for 5 minutes. Remove from heat and stir in cheese, breadcrumbs, herbs, orange rind, salt and pepper.

2 Leave to cool slightly then stir in the beaten egg until evenly combined. Shape mixture into 2.5 cm (1 in) balls. Heat remaining 2 tablespoons oil in a frying pan and fry stuffing balls for about 10 minutes, turning frequently, until golden then drain.

3 To make the pie, trim leeks and cut into 1 cm (½ in) chunks. Cut turnips into chunks and thickly slice carrots. Heat oil in a large saucepan and fry leeks, turnips and carrots for 3 minutes.

4 Stir in the flour, then gradually blend in wine and stock. Add bay leaves and bring to the boil. Reduce heat, cover and simmer for 15 minutes, until vegetables are softened.

5 Meanwhile, thickly slice parsnip. Add parsnip, mushrooms and chestnuts to pan. Season with salt and pepper then leave to cool.

6 Using a slotted spoon, turn the vegetables into a large, deep pie dish. Arrange the stuffing balls over vegetables. Pour over enough of the juices to two-thirds fill dish. (Keep any remaining juices to reheat and serve separately).

7 Preheat oven to 200C (400F/Gas 6). Roll out pastry on a lightly floured surface to a round or oval 7.5 cm (3 in) larger than pie dish. Cut a 2.5 cm (1 in) wide strip from outside edge of pastry.

8 Dampen rim of dish and position strip on rim. Brush strip with water. Position pastry lid, pressing edges together to seal and making a small hole in centre of pastry. Flute edges decoratively. Make leaves from the pastry trimmings and use to garnish the top of the pie.

9 Brush with beaten egg and bake for 25 minutes. Reduce oven temperature to 160C (325F/Gas 3). Bake for a further 30 minutes, covering with foil if over-browning. Serve hot.

COOK'S TIP

If you want extra gravy, make the Roast Onion Gravy on page 45. Cranberry sauce is also delicious with this pie.

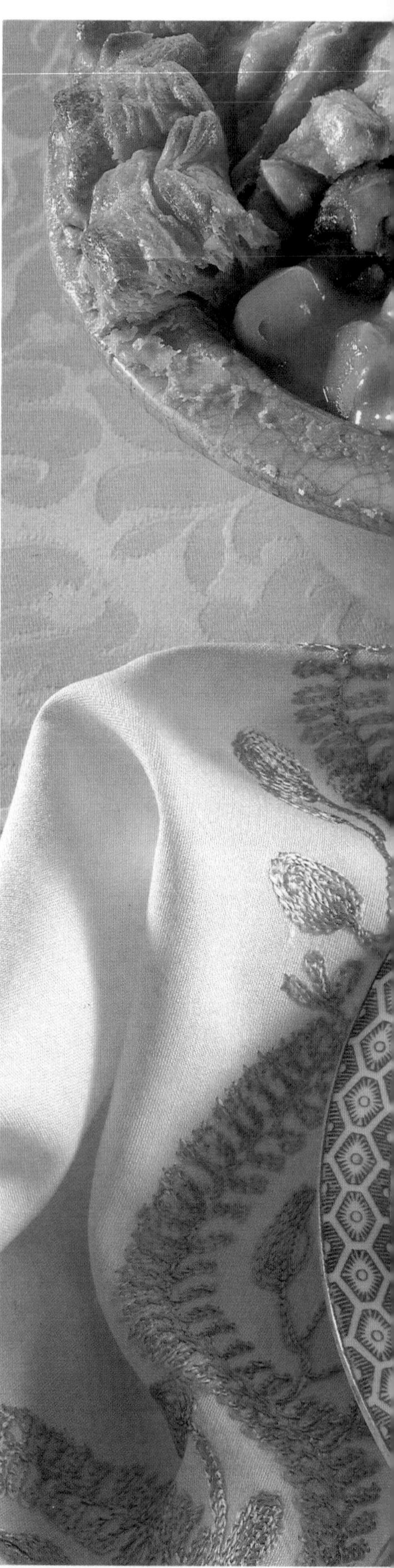

ROAST LENTIL PATTIES

SERVES 4

1 large leek
2 courgettes
4 tablespoons olive oil
280 g (9 oz) split red lentils
450 ml (¾ pint) vegetable stock
90 g (3 oz) broken walnuts
2 tablespoons double cream
1 tablespoon chopped fresh rosemary
1 egg, beaten
salt
1 tablespoon crushed peppercorns
rosemary sprigs, to garnish

1 Finely chop and wash leek. Grate the courgettes. Heat 3 tablespoons of oil in a saucepan. Add leek and courgettes and fry for 3 minutes. Add lentils and stock and bring to the boil. Reduce heat, cover tightly with lid and simmer for 10–15 minutes, until mixture is thick and pulpy. Leave to cool.

2 Preheat oven to 200C (400F/Gas 6). Toast walnuts on a sheet of foil under the grill, turning them frequently. Leave to cool then roughly chop. Beat walnuts, cream, rosemary, egg and salt into the lentil mixture.

3 Using lightly floured hands, shape mixture into 12 balls and flatten slightly.

4 Sprinkle with peppercorns and place in a baking dish. Drizzle with remaining 1 tablespoon oil. Bake for 20–25 minutes, until crispy. Serve hot garnished with sprigs of rosemary.

AUBERGINE AND FETA TART

SERVES 8

1 medium aubergine, weighing about 315 g (10 oz)
2 onions
8 tablespoons olive oil
60 g (2 oz) sun dried tomatoes
2 small courgettes
125 g (4 oz) feta cheese
½ teaspoon mild chilli seasoning
salt
6 sheets of filo pastry

1 Preheat oven to 190C (375F/Gas 5). Cut the aubergine into dice. Slice the onions. Heat 4 tablespoons of the oil in a large frying pan. Add aubergine and onion and fry gently for 8–10 minutes, until golden.

2 Roughly chop the tomatoes and courgettes. Add to the pan and cook for a further 2 minutes. Lightly crumble in the feta cheese and stir in chilli seasoning. Add salt to taste.

3 Line a 23 cm (9 in) loose-bottomed flan tin with a sheet of the filo pastry, tucking pastry into corners and letting excess overhang edges. Brush pastry within tin area with a little oil.

4 Lay another sheet of pastry over first but in opposite direction. Brush with more oil. Continue lining tin with remaining filo sheets, brushing each with oil and alternating direction of sheets so that the pastry overhanging edges is evenly distributed.

5 Spoon filling into tin and spread to edges. Crumple the excess pastry around the edges of the tin to give an attractive border. Brush with remaining oil.

6 Bake for 20–25 minutes or until golden. Serve warm or cold.

ROAST ONION GRAVY

MAKES 600 ML (1 PINT)

500 g (1 lb) onions
2 garlic cloves
2 tablespoons olive oil
2 bay leaves
few drops of soy sauce
750 ml ($1\frac{1}{4}$ pints) vegetable stock
$1\frac{1}{2}$ teaspoons cornflour

1 Preheat oven to 200C (400F/Gas 6). Slice onions and garlic, leaving skins on. Put in an ovenproof dish and drizzle with olive oil. Bake for 1 hour, until lightly charred.

2 Transfer to a saucepan and add bay leaves, soy sauce and vegetable stock. Simmer for 15 minutes.

3 Strain through a sieve, reserving a few onion slices.

4 In a saucepan, blend cornflour with a little of the strained stock. Gradually blend in remaining stock and reserved onion slices. Bring to the boil, stirring until thickened.

COOK'S TIP

It's the addition of onion skins that provide the golden colour of this vegetarian gravy – a technique worth remembering for vegetarian stocks, soups and gravy.

POLENTA
WITH SAFFRON MUSHROOMS

SERVES 4

1½ teaspoons salt
280 g (9 oz) polenta
125 g (4 oz) freshly grated Parmesan cheese
3 tablespoons olive oil
1 teaspoon saffron strands
1 onion
3 celery sticks
1 red pepper
45 g (1½ oz) pine nuts
125 g (4 oz) shitake mushrooms
180 g (6 oz) button mushrooms
300 ml (½ pint) double cream
salt and pepper
Chilli Tomato Sauce, see opposite

1 Bring 1.1 litre (2 pints) water to the boil in a large saucepan. Add the salt. Gradually whisk in the polenta until thickened. When thick and pulpy, reduce heat and cook very gently for 10 minutes, stirring frequently with a wooden spoon. Beat in half the cheese.
2 Turn polenta into a greased flameproof dish and spread to an even layer, about 2.5 cm (1 in) thick. Drizzle with 1 tablespoon of the oil and sprinkle with remaining cheese.
3 Mix saffron strands with 1 tablespoon boiling water and set aside.
4 Slice the onion and chop the celery. Cut the pepper in half, discard core and seeds and slice the flesh. Heat remaining oil in a saucepan and add onion, celery and pine nuts. Cook gently, stirring, until softened.
5 Add red pepper and mushrooms and cook for a further 2 minutes. Stir in saffron and liquid, cream, salt and pepper. Heat gently.
6 Cook polenta under a moderate grill until hot and turning golden. Cut into portions. Spoon mushroom mixture on to warmed serving plates and top with portions of polenta. Serve with the Chilli Tomato Sauce.

POLENTA

Polenta is a type of flour, ground from corn or maize, that is particularly popular in Italian cookery. Look for it in Italian delicatessens and large supermarkets. Polenta is not difficult to make but because it tends to spit and splutter during cooking, it is best to use a tall, heavy-based saucepan and a long-handled wooden spoon. It is also important to stir the mixture frequently to prevent lumps forming.

Polenta is usually flavoured with cheese, herbs or garlic then grilled and cut into wedges. It can also be served as an alternative to pasta, rice or potatoes. Simply simmer it in the water until pulpy then season lightly and serve plain or beat in ...il butter, garlic, ground ... herbs as

CHILLI TOMATO SAUCE

SERVES 6

1 red pepper
1 chilli
375 g (12 oz) tomatoes
1 onion
1 garlic clove
3 tablespoons olive oil
1 tablespoon tomato purée
pinch of sugar
salt and pepper

1 Preheat oven to 200C (400F/Gas 6). Cut pepper into quarters, discarding core and seeds. Halve chilli, discard core and seeds and ...ughly chop flesh. Halve the tomatoes and slice the onions.

2 Put pepper, chilli, tomatoes, onion and garlic in an ovenproof dish and drizzle with the oil. Bake for 1 hour, until vegetables are lightly charred.

3 Blend vegetables in a food processor until pulpy but not completely smooth. Turn into a saucepan.

4 Stir in tomato purée, sugar, salt and pepper and reheat gently before serving.

COOK'S TIP

When preparing fresh chillies, handle them as little as possible as the volatile oils in the flesh can give your skin a burning or tingling sensation. Rinse your hands well afterwards.

SMOKED MACKEREL AND ROCKET TERRINE

SERVES 12

375 g (12 oz) smoked mackerel
90 g (3 oz) butter
1 tablespoon white wine vinegar
pepper
375 g (12 oz) cream cheese
60 g (2 oz) rocket
grated rind of 1 lemon
200 g (7 oz) can pimientos, drained
melba toast or toast, to serve

1 Discard skin from fish and roughly flake the flesh. Melt the butter. Put the fish, butter, vinegar and pepper in a food processor and blend until smooth and creamy. (Alternatively mash ingredients together in a bowl).
2 Beat cream cheese in a bowl. Finely chop rocket and add to bowl with lemon rind, salt and pepper. Beat well together.
3 Cut 3 wide strips from one of the pimientos. Open out remaining pimientos pieces.
4 Spoon half the mackerel mixture into a small rectangular terrine. Spread with half the cheese mixture. Cover with half the pimiento pieces. Spread with remaining mackerel mixture and add remaining pimiento pieces. Spread with remaining cheese mixture and swirl the surface.
5 Garnish with the pimiento strips. Chill for several hours or overnight. Serve with melba toast or fingers of toast.

COOK'S TIP

If you can't buy pimientos, use 3 red peppers. Halve, discard the cores and seeds then simmer in water for 15 minutes.

TABBOULEH WITH NECTARINES

SERVES 8

250 g (8 oz) bulghur wheat (burgul)
1 orange pepper
2 garlic cloves
4 tablespoons chopped fresh mint
4 tablespoons chopped fresh parsley
$\frac{1}{2}$ teaspoon ground allspice
grated rind and juice of 1 small orange
4 tablespoons extra virgin olive oil
salt and pepper
4 nectarines
fresh herbs such as mint, parsley or bay leaves, to garnish

1 Put bulghur wheat in a bowl, cover with plenty of boiling water and leave to stand for 20 minutes. Drain thoroughly and turn into a bowl.
2 Meanwhile, cut the pepper in half, discarding core and seeds and finely chop the flesh. Crush the garlic.
3 Add pepper, garlic, mint, parsley, allspice, orange rind and juice, oil, salt and pepper to the bulghur wheat and toss well together until thoroughly combined.
4 Halve nectarines and remove stones. Take a slice off rounded side of each half so that it sits flat.
5 Pile the salad mixture into the fruit halves and arrange on a serving plate. Cover loosely and chill in the refrigerator until ready to serve. Garnish with fresh herbs.

COOK'S TIP

If preferred, the fruit can be added to the salad. Use 2 nectarines, thinly sliced, and toss gently with the other ingredients.

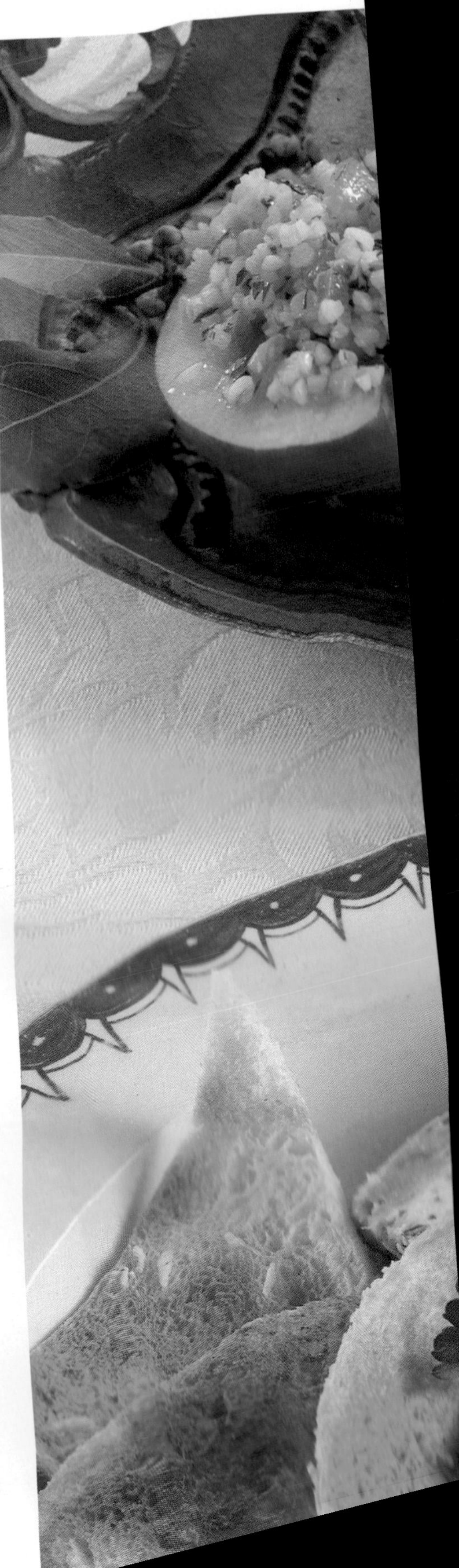

NEW POTATO SALAD

SERVES 8

750 g ($1\frac{1}{2}$ lb) small new potatoes
salt and pepper
125 g (4 oz) sprouting broccoli
4 spring onions
4 tablespoons pine nuts
5 tablespoons olive oil
1 tablespoon white wine vinegar
good pinch of caster sugar

1 Wash potatoes and put in a saucepan. Cover with boiling water, add salt and cook for about 15 minutes, until just tender.
2 Meanwhile, cut the broccoli into bite-sized pieces and lay over the potatoes. Cover and cook for a further 2 minutes, until broccoli is tender. Drain the vegetables and set aside.
3 Finely slice spring onions and put in a small pan with the pine nuts and 2 tablespoons of the oil. Cook gently, shaking pan until pine nuts are toasted. Mix in a bowl with the potatoes and broccoli.
4 Mix together the remaining olive oil, the vinegar, sugar, salt and pepper. Pour over the salad and toss lightly together. Chill in the refrigerator until ready to serve.

COOK'S TIP

Even though this is a cold salad, it is best to pour the dressing over the cooked potatoes whilst they are still warm, as this allows the flavours to be absorbed.

SPICED COLESLAW WITH AVOCADO

SERVES 8

$\frac{1}{2}$ small onion
grated rind and juice of 1 lime
2 tablespoons roughly chopped fresh coriander
$\frac{1}{2}$ teaspoon curry paste
$\frac{1}{2}$ teaspoon paprika
2 tablespoons mayonnaise
375 g (12 oz) green cabbage
60 g (2 oz) Palma or Serrano ham
salt and pepper
1 ripe avocado
fresh coriander, to garnish

1 Grate the onion and put in a large bowl with the lime rind and juice, coriander, curry paste, paprika and mayonnaise. Mix together to make a smooth dressing.

2 Using a sharp knife, finely shred the cabbage and stir into the dressing. Tear or slice the ham into small pieces and add to the salad. Toss ingredients together and season lightly with salt and pepper. Chill in the refrigerator until ready to serve.

3 Just before serving, halve avocado, discarding stone. Peel away skin and slice the flesh widthways. Add to the salad, toss together and serve garnished with coriander.

COOK'S TIP

Any leftover cooked meats can be substituted in this recipe, for the same quantity of ham.

PASTA, ARTICHOKE AND WALNUT SALAD

SERVES 8

375 g (12 oz) penne pasta
salt and pepper
4 tablespoons walnut oil
400 g (14 oz) can artichoke hearts
125 g (4 oz) cherry tomatoes
90 g (3 oz) broken walnuts
60 g (2 oz) black olives
grated rind and juice of 1 lemon
60 g (2 oz) Parmesan cheese
flat-leaved parsley, to garnish

1 Cook pasta in plenty of boiling salted water for 8–10 minutes, until tender. Drain and toss in a bowl with 1 tablespoon of the oil.

2 Drain artichoke hearts and cut in half. Cut tomatoes in half and add to pasta with artichokes, walnuts and olives.

3 Mix lemon rind and juice with remaining oil, salt and pepper. Add to bowl and toss ingredients lightly together. Chill until ready to serve.

4 Using a potato peeler, pare Parmesan cheese into shavings. Turn salad into a serving dish and sprinkle with the cheese and chopped parsley.

COOK'S TIP

Instead of penne, other short cut or small pasta shapes could be used in this salad. Varieties include conchiglie, which are in the shape of seashells, farfalle, in the shape of bow-ties and fusilli which are spiral shaped pasta. As with all pasta, don't over-cook as it will become limp and soft.

TOMATO AND PEPPER SALAD

SERVES 8

½ a small cucumber
½ a small red skinned onion
1 red chilli
1 tablespoon capers
1 tablespoon wholegrain mustard
2 teaspoons white wine vinegar
1 teaspoon caster sugar
5 tablespoons olive oil
salt and pepper
2 beefsteak tomatoes
4 plum or small tomatoes
180 g (6 oz) cherry tomatoes
1 yellow pepper
1 red or orange pepper
parsley to garnish, if desired

1 Finely dice cucumber. Finely chop onion. Halve the chilli, discarding the core and seeds and finely chop the flesh.
2 Mix together the cucumber, onion, chilli, capers, mustard, vinegar, sugar, 3 tablespoons of the oil, salt and pepper.
3 Slice beefsteak tomatoes and arrange, overlapping, on a serving plate. Cut plum tomatoes into wedges and halve cherry tomatoes. Arrange the plum and cherry tomatoes on the plate.
4 Cut peppers in half, discarding cores and seeds and chop the flesh into small chunks. Scatter them over the tomatoes. Cover and chill in the refrigerator until ready to serve.
5 Spoon remaining oil over the salad and season with salt and pepper. Spoon the sauce over the top and serve garnished with fresh parsley, if desired.

COOK'S TIP

To avoid last minute preparation, chop the vegetables a day in advance and prepare the dressing, ready for assembling before serving. For a more substantial salad, scatter diced or crumbled feta cheese over the top of the salad. Alternatively, arrange slices of mozzarella cheese between the slices of beefsteak tomatoes, on the serving plate.

SAUSAGE, APPLE AND MUSTARD ROLLS

MAKES ABOUT 28

450 g (14 oz) pork sausagemeat
2 dessert apples
2 teaspoons Dijon mustard
salt and pepper
500 g (1 lb) puff pastry
beaten egg, to glaze

1 Preheat oven to 220C (425F/ Gas 7). Lightly grease 2 baking sheets.

2 Beat sausagemeat in a bowl. Peel, core and grate apples and add to bowl with the mustard, salt and pepper. Beat well to combine.

3 Halve the pastry. On a lightly floured surface, roll out one half to a 38×25.5 cm (15×10 in) rectangle. Cut lengthways into 2 strips. Divide sausagemeat into 4 equal pieces. Spoon a quarter down 1 strip and another quarter down remaining strip.

4 Brush edges of pastry with beaten egg then bring pastry over filling, sealing long edges together. Trim and flute edges neatly.

5 Brush with beaten egg to glaze then cut into 5 cm (2 in) lengths. Score tops with a knife and transfer to baking sheets. Make more rolls with remaining pastry and the sausagemeat filling.

6 Bake for 25–30 minutes, until risen and golden. Transfer to a wire rack to cool.

COOK'S TIPS

If preferred, these rolls can be made using shortcrust pastry. Rub 90 g (3 oz) butter or margarine and 90 g (3 oz) lard into 350 g (12 oz) plain flour then add enough cold water to make a firm dough. Chill for 30 minutes before rolling out as above.

If made with fresh pastry and sausagemeat, these rolls can be frozen before cooking. Bake from frozen, allowing a few minutes extra.

Puddings

Rich Christmas Pudding

Makes two 1.1 litre (2 pint) puddings, each serving 8–10

125 g (4 oz) blanched almonds
60 g (2 oz) pecan or walnut halves
60 g (2 oz) glacé cherries
250 g (8 oz) dried figs or dates
60 g (2 oz) mixed peel
175 g (6 oz) fresh breadcrumbs
250 g (8 oz) sultanas
375 g (12 oz) raisins
375 g (12 oz) currants
125 g (4 oz) shredded vegetable suet
125 g (4 oz) self raising flour
1 cooking apple
grated rind and juice of 2 oranges
3 eggs, lightly beaten
1 teaspoon ground cinnamon
1 teaspoon ground ginger
6 tablespoons ginger wine or ale

1 Lightly grease and base line two 1.1 litre (2 pint) pudding basins.
2 Roughly chop almonds, pecan or walnuts, cherries and figs or dates and put in a large bowl. Add the mixed peel, breadcrumbs, sultanas, raisins, currants, suet and flour and stir until evenly combined.
3 Peel and grate the apple and add to the bowl with the orange rind and juice, eggs, cinnamon, ginger and ginger wine or ale. Stir well until the mixture is sticky. Divide mixture between the basins and pack down lightly.
4 Pleat a piece of greased greaseproof paper and foil together and lay over one basin, tying securely with string under the rim. Do the same on other pudding.
5 Stand puddings on steaming racks or old, upturned saucers and place in large saucepans. (Alternatively use a large double saucepan). Pour in enough boiling water to come a good third up sides of basins. Cover and simmer for 4 hours, topping up water level when necessary.
6 Remove puddings from pans and leave to cool for 1–2 hours. Re-cover with fresh greaseproof paper and foil. Store in a cool, dark place for at least 1 month (or up to 1 year) before serving.
7 To reheat Christmas pudding, steam as above for about 2 hours.

Brandy Butter

SERVES 6–8

125 g (4 oz) unsalted butter
45 g (1½ oz) icing sugar
2 tablespoons brandy

1 Soften butter and put in a food processor with the icing sugar and brandy. Mix until smooth and creamy. (Alternatively, in a bowl, beat together butter and icing sugar until evenly combined. Add brandy and mix until absorbed).
2 Turn into a small serving dish and chill until required.

Whipped Amaretto Butter

SERVES 6

30 g (1 oz) amaretti or macaroon biscuits
60 g (2 oz) unsalted butter
75 ml (3fl oz) double cream
1 tablespoon amaretto liqueur
cinnamon, for dusting

1 Put biscuits in a polythene bag and crush with a rolling pin until completely ground.
2 Beat butter in a bowl until softened. Add biscuits and beat together. Add cream and liqueur and whip lightly until thickened.
3 Turn into a small serving dish and dust with cinnamon. Chill until required.

Marmalade Butter

SERVES 6–8

1 slice of day old bread
125 g (4 oz) unsalted butter
3 tablespoons orange or lemon shredded marmalade
thin strips of orange or lemon zest, to decorate

1 Toast the bread and crumble into small pieces.
2 Beat butter in a bowl until softened. Add the marmalade and beat together until well mixed.
3 Turn into a small serving dish and chill until required. Serve sprinkled with the crumbled toast and strips of zest.

EGG CUSTARD

SERVES 6–8

750 ml (24fl oz) milk
3 tablespoons caster sugar
1 tablespoon cornflour
2 eggs
pinch of salt
1½ teaspoons vanilla essence

1 Pour milk into a saucepan and bring to the boil over gentle heat. Meanwhile, beat together sugar, cornflour, eggs and salt in a bowl.
2 Whisk about 60 ml (2fl oz) of boiling milk into egg mixture. Return to saucepan.
3 Continue cooking over gentle heat, beating all the time with a wooden spoon until custard is smooth and thick. Simmer for 1 minute, still beating. Remove from heat and stir in vanilla essence.

STEP 1

STEP 2

ORANGE AND BRANDY BUTTER

SERVES 6–8

125 g (4 oz) unsalted butter
155 g (5 oz) icing sugar
2 teaspoons grated orange rind
1 tablespoon brandy or rum

1 Beat butter in bowl until softened. Cream the butter with an electric whisk or wooden spoon until very light and fluffy.
2 Gradually beat in icing sugar and continue beating until mixture is white in colour. Beat in orange rind, then brandy or rum. Cover with plastic wrap and chill in the refrigerator until required.

STEP 1

STEP 2

CLEAR BRANDY SAUCE

SERVES 6–8

90 g (3 oz) soft brown sugar
2 tablespoons cornflour
pinch of salt
500 ml (16fl oz) water
2.5 cm (1 in) cinnamon stick
6 whole cloves
30 g (1 oz) butter
60 ml (2fl oz) brandy

1 Combine brown sugar, cornflour and salt in a medium saucepan. Gradually stir in water.
2 Place over moderate heat and add cinnamon stick and cloves. Bring to the boil, stirring. Reduce heat and simmer for 3 minutes. Remove cinnamon and cloves. Stir in butter and enough brandy to give desired flavour. Serve hot.

STEP 1

STEP 2

ANGEL'S GATEAU

SERVES 10–12

8 egg whites
good pinch of salt
1 teaspoon cream of tartar
2 teaspoons vanilla essence
315 g (10 oz) caster sugar
180 g (6 oz) plain flour
250 g (8 oz) mascarpone cheese
300 ml (½ pint) double cream
2 tablespoons icing sugar
3 tablespoons Kirsch
1 star fruit
1 pomegranate
1 small honeydew or galia melon
1 pawpaw
small bunch of seedless grapes
small piece of fresh coconut

★

1 Preheat oven to 170C (325F/Gas 3). Brush a 2 litre (3 pint) deep ring tin with oil. Coat base and sides with flour and shake out excess.

2 In a large bowl, whisk egg whites until holding their shape. Add salt and cream of tartar and whisk again until stiff.

3 Add vanilla essence and whisk in 1 tablespoon of the sugar. Continue adding sugar, a tablespoon at a time, whisking well after each addition until glossy.

4 Sift flour over egg whites and carefully fold in. Turn into tin and level surface. Bake for about 45 minutes until a skewer, inserted into centre, comes out clean.

5 Invert on to a wire rack and leave to cool. Transfer to a serving plate.

6 Beat together mascarpone cheese, cream, icing sugar and Kirsch until mixture stands in peaks. Spread all over cake.

7 Thinly slice star fruit. Remove and separate pomegranate seeds. Halve and remove seeds from melon then scoop out flesh with a melon baller. Halve pawpaw and scoop out seeds. Peel away skin and slice flesh. Remove grapes from stalk.

8 Use half the fruit to fill centre of ring. Pile remainder attractively on top of gateau. Using a potato peeler, pare strips of coconut and scatter over the fruits. Chill until ready to serve.

COOK'S TIP

This cake can be made well in advance and frozen before decorating. If preferred, substitute an orange flavoured liqueur or rum for the Kirsch.

CHRISTMAS ROULADE

SERVES 8

280 g (9 oz) plain chocolate
1 piece of stem ginger plus 2 tablespoons syrup
4 eggs, separated
125 g (4 oz) caster sugar
600 ml (1 pint) double cream
60 g (2 oz) milk chocolate polka dots
1 Flake bar
2 bags of gold chocolate coins
cocoa powder, for dusting

★

1 Preheat oven to 180C (350F/Gas 4). Grease and line a 30 × 20 cm (12 × 8 in) Swiss roll tin with greaseproof paper.
[illegible] up 125 g (4 oz) of the chocolate and put in a bowl. Stand the bowl over a saucepan of simmering water. Leave until melted, stirring frequently.
3 Finely chop the ginger. Whisk together egg yolks and sugar until pale and creamy. Fold the melted chocolate into the creamed mixture with the ginger and syrup.
4 Whisk egg whites until they stand in peaks. Using a metal spoon, fold a quarter into chocolate mixture. Carefully fold in remainder.
5 Spread the mixture evenly into the prepared tin and bake for 15–20 minutes, until just firm. Cover with a tea-towel to prevent the roulade from drying out and leave to cool for about 20 minutes.
6 Whip 300 ml ($\frac{1}{2}$ pint) of the cream and fold in polka dots. Turn roulade out of tin on to a sheet of greaseproof paper and peel away paper. Spread with the cream mixture. Roll up the roulade carefully but do not roll up too tightly and do not worry if it cracks. Transfer to a rectangular plate or cake board. Cut log in half widthways then open out slightly as though broken in half.
7 Break up remaining chocolate and put in a saucepan with the remaining cream. Heat gently until chocolate has melted. Chill.
8 Whip the chocolate mixture until just beginning to stand in peaks then spread over both the logs. Break up the Flake bar and scatter over top.
9 Scatter coins between and in front of logs, then dust generously with cocoa powder.
10 Store the Yule Log in an airtight tin for up to 3 days.

SPICY PECAN PUDDINGS

MAKES 8–10

150 g (5 oz) butter
180 g (6 oz) caster sugar
¼ teaspoon ground cinnamon
¼ teaspoon ground mixed spice
5 eggs, separated
30 g (1 oz) plain flour
2 tablespoons cocoa powder
2 tablespoons lemon juice
60 g (2 oz) pecan nuts
125 g (4 oz) ground almonds
60 g (2 oz) fresh breadcrumbs
holly leaves, pecan nuts and cranberries, to decorate
creme fraiche or Greek yogurt and maple syrup, to serve

★

1 Preheat oven to 180C (350F/Gas 4). Grease 10 dariole moulds or 8 individual pudding tins and line bases with greaseproof paper.

2 Beat butter in a bowl until softened. Add 60 g (2 oz) of the sugar, the cinnamon and mixed spice and beat together until fluffy. Add egg yolks, flour, cocoa powder and lemon juice and gently stir in. Chop pecan nuts and stir into mixture with the ground almonds and breadcrumbs until just combined.

3 In a separate bowl, whisk egg whites until stiff. Gradually whisk in remaining sugar.

4 Fold a quarter into the pecan mixture to lighten. Carefully fold in remainder until just incorporated. Three-quarters fill the prepared tins.

5 Arrange in a roasting tin and pour a 2.5 cm (1 in) depth of boiling water into the tin. Cover completely with foil and bake for 30 minutes, until puddings feel firm.

6 Loosen edges and turn out on to serving plates. Decorate with holly leaves, pecan nuts and cranberries. Spoon a little creme fraiche or yogurt beside the puddings and pour over a little maple syrup.

COOK'S TIPS

For convenience, make the puddings in advance and freeze, uncooked. Bake from frozen allowing an extra 5 minutes. As an alternative to the creme fraiche or Greek yogurt, the Hot Apricot Sauce on page 65 or the Rich Chocolate Sauce on next page, both make delicious accompaniments to the

Rich Vanilla Custard

SERVES 8

30 g (1 oz) caster sugar
1 tablespoon cornflour
2 eggs
2 teaspoons vanilla essence
600 ml (1 pint) milk

1 Beat together the sugar, cornflour, eggs and vanilla essence, until smooth.
2 Pour milk into a saucepan and bring just to the boil. Immediately pour over the egg mixture, stirring.
3 Return custard to pan and cook very gently, stirring with a wooden spoon, until custard [illegible] boil. Serve hot.

Sweet Sauces

Sweet sauces make the perfect accompaniment to various hot and cold desserts and keep well in the refrigerator for 2–3 days. They can also be used decoratively as a base on which to serve individual portions of dessert. Spoon a little sauce on to the plates and tap or tilt the plates until the sauce is level. Using a teaspoon, drizzle a little single or double cream over the sauce and, using a cocktail stick or the tip of a skewer, swirl the cream into the sauce to give a pretty feathered finish. Carefully arrange the dessert on the sauce and decorate with sprigs of mint. Serve immediately.

Rich Chocolate Sauce

SERVES 6

180 g (6 oz) plain chocolate
30 g (1 oz) unsalted butter
4 tablespoons golden syrup
150 ml (5fl oz) milk

1 Break up chocolate and put in a small saucepan with the butter, syrup and milk.
2 Cook gently, stirring, until smooth and glossy. Serve warm or cold.

Cook's Tip

Serve this sauce with hot puddings or use it to dress up vanilla ice-cream. If it over thickens on cooling, beat in a little extra milk.

EASY CHRISTMAS PUDDING

SERVES 6

125 g (4 oz) butter or margarine
90 g (3 oz) soft brown sugar
2 eggs
185 g (6 oz) self-raising flour
1 teaspoon mixed spice
pinch of salt
155 g (5oz) mixed dried fruit
75 g (2 ½ oz) chopped dates
45 g (1 ½ oz) halved glacé cherries
4 tablespoons sherry or orange juice
Fluffy Pineapple Sauce to serve, see right

1 Grease a 1 litre (32fl oz) pudding basin. Cream butter or margarine and sugar in a bowl until light and fluffy. Add eggs and beat well.
2 Sift flour with spice and salt. Fold into creamed mixture.
3 Add mixed fruit, dates, cherries and sherry or orange juice and mix well.
4 Spoon mixture into prepared pudding basin and cover with a tight-fitting lid or pleat a piece of greased greaseproof paper and foil together and lay over the basin, tying securely with string under the rim.
5 Stand pudding on a steaming rack or old upturned saucer and place in a large saucepan. (Alternatively use a large double saucepan.) Pour in enough boiling water to come a good third up sides of basin. Cover and simmer briskly for 2 hours, topping up water level when necessary.
6 Turn out pudding onto a warmed serving plate and pour a little Fluffy Pineapple Sauce over the top. Serve the remaining sauce separately.

PUDDING: STEP 1

STEP 2

STEP 3

STEP 4

FLUFFY PINEAPPLE SAUCE

SERVES 6

2 eggs, separated
1½ tablespoons lemon juice
4 tablespoons cornflour
845 ml (27fl oz) unsweetened pineapple juice
4 tablespoons brown sugar

1 Beat together the egg yolks, lemon juice and cornflour until smooth.
2 Pour pineapple juice and brown sugar into a saucepan and heat to simmering point. Gradually stir in the cornflour mixture and continue stirring over low heat until mixture is smooth and thickened. Simmer for 2 minutes. Remove from heat and cool. Pour into a bowl.
3 In a large bowl, whisk egg whites until stiff and fold into pineapple sauce using a metal spoon. Serve immediately, or cover and chill until required, then reheat gently.

COOK'S TIP

If you have any left over, this light, tangy sauce is also delicious served chilled with

SUGAR AND SPICE PAVLOVA

SERVES 8

5 egg whites
315 g (10 oz) caster sugar
2 teaspoons cornflour
1 teaspoon ground mixed spice
2 teaspoons white wine vinegar
600 ml (1 pint) double cream
2 tablespoons creme de cassis
250 g (8 oz) cape gooseberries
3 figs
250–375 g (8–12 oz) mixed soft fruits such as strawberries, blueberries, raspberries
icing sugar and cinnamon, to dust

1 Preheat oven to 150C (300F/Gas 2). Draw a 20 cm (8 in) circle on to a piece of non-stick baking parchment, and an 18 cm (7 in) circle on to another. Use to line 2 baking sheets.

2 In a bowl, whisk egg whites until stiff. Gradually whisk in the sugar, a tablespoon at a time, whisking well between each addition until stiff and glossy. Sift in the cornflour and spice and fold in with the vinegar.

3 Spread two-thirds of the meringue almost to edge of the larger circle. Use remainder to spread over smaller circle.

4 Bake for 5 minutes then reduce oven temperature to 130C (250F/Gas $\frac{1}{2}$) and bake for a further hour or until crisp. Leave to cool on a wire rack then carefully peel off the paper.

5 Whip cream with creme de cassis until just beginning to stand in peaks. Remove skins from half the gooseberries. Open out skins on remainder and reserve for decorating. Cut the figs into wedges.

6 Lay the large meringue on a serving plate. Spread with half the cream and cover with half of the skinned gooseberries and half of the figs.

7 Add

cover with remaining cream. Decorate with remaining fruits. Just before serving, dust with sifted icing sugar and cinnamon.

COOK'S TIPS

Make sure you spread the meringue on to non-stick baking parchment as greaseproof paper does not always come away easily from the cooked meringue.

Avoid assembling more than 1–2 hours before serving as the pavlova will gradually soften.

HOT *APRICOT* *SAUCE*

SERVES 6

225 g (8 oz) ripe apricots
30 g (1 oz) caster sugar
2 teaspoons lemon or lime juice
2 tablespoons brandy

1 Halve and stone apricots. Put in a saucepan with the sugar and 50 ml (2fl oz) water.

2 Simmer gently for about 5 minutes, until apricots are completely soft. Cool slightly then blend in a food processor.

3 Return to pan and stir in the lemon or lime juice and brandy. Heat through gently and serve hot or chill and serve cold.

COOK'S TIPS

This sauce can also be made with other fruits, such as plums, gooseberries, peaches, strawberries and redcurrants, although you may need to adjust the quantity of sugar depending on the sweetness of the fruit used. If using raspberries or blackberries, after blending, press them through a sieve to remove the seeds.

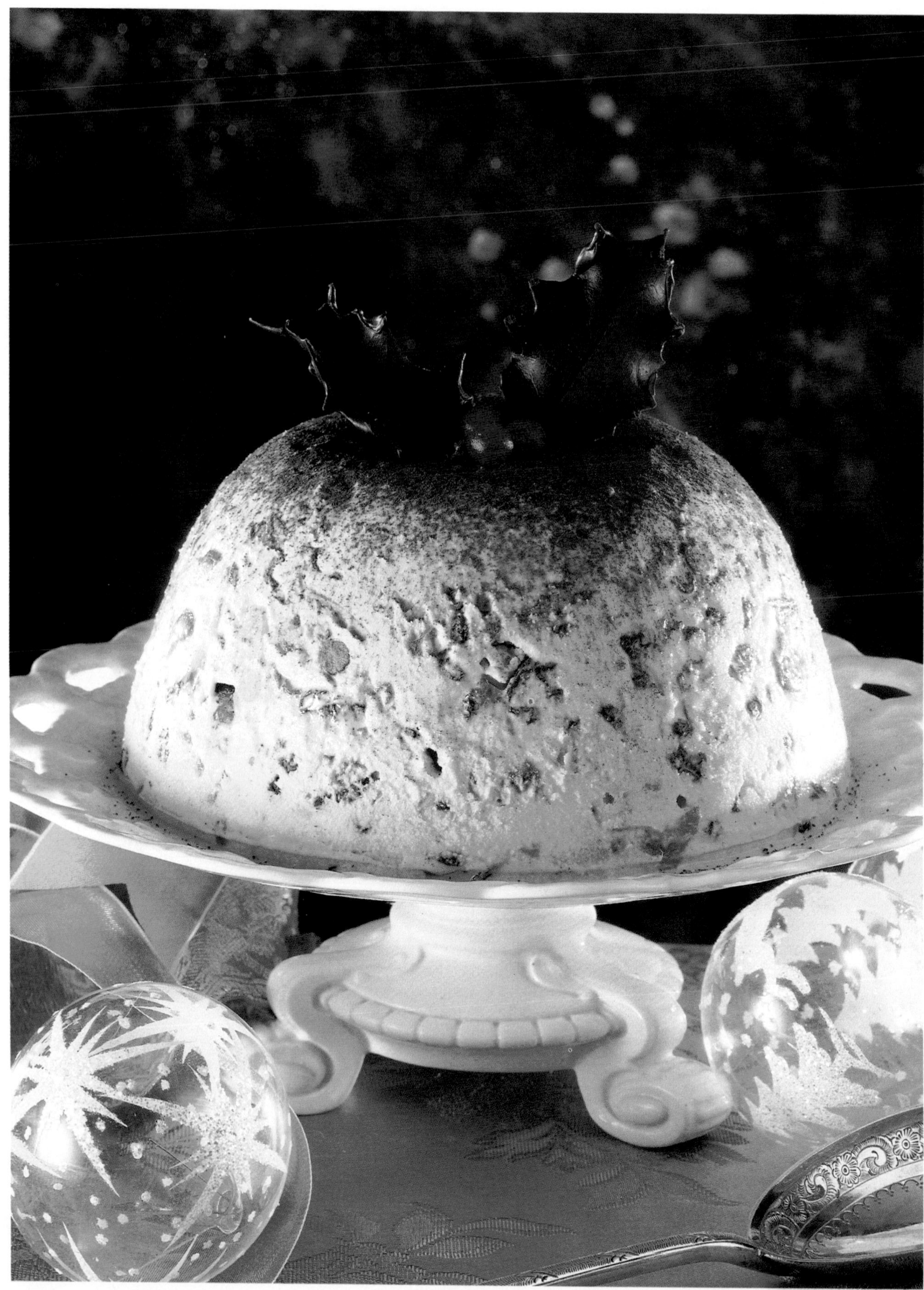

ICED CHRISTMAS PUDDING

SERVES 10–12

60 g (2 oz) sultanas
60 g (2 oz) currants
60 g (2 oz) raisins
125 g (4 oz) chopped glacé cherries
60 g (2 oz) chopped mixed dried peel
30 g (1 oz) chopped glacé pineapple or stem ginger
60 ml (2fl oz) brandy
125 g (4 oz) flaked almonds
1 litre (32fl oz) vanilla ice-cream
155 ml (5fl oz) double cream
60 g (2 oz) chocolate chips
sieved cocoa powder, chocolate holly leaves and marzipan berries, to decorate, see Cook's Tips

1 Mix dried fruits with brandy. Cover with plastic wrap and leave for several hours.

2 Toast almonds under a grill, stirring frequently until golden. Soften ice-cream and place in a bowl with cream. Stir in fruits, almonds and chocolate chips.

3 Spoon into a 1.75 litre (3 pint) pudding basin and cover with freezer wrap. Freeze overnight.

4 Remove freezer wrap and immerse basin in hot water for 20 seconds. Unmould pudding onto a chilled serving plate and decorate.

PUDDING: STEP 1

STEP 2

STEP 3

COOK'S TIP

To make chocolate leaves, wash and dry several holly leaves. Brush backs of leaves with melted chocolate and refrigerate, chocolate side up, on a baking sheet lined with non-stick baking paper. When chocolate is set, carefully peel leaves off chocolate. The holly berries are made from balls of red marzipan. If you would like a dark pudding, simply use chocolate ice-cream in place of vanilla. Strawberry ice-cream would create a pretty pink pudding.

APRICOT SHERRY TRIFLE

SERVES 6–8

440 g (14 oz) pkt sponge rolls
125 ml (4fl oz) sweet sherry, Marsala or port
two 411 g ($14\frac{1}{2}$ oz) cans apricot halves, drained
500 ml (16fl oz) prepared custard
142 g (4 oz) packet raspberry or strawberry jelly made up according to instructions and set in a shallow tin
300 ml ($\frac{1}{2}$ pint) double cream
fresh fruit and chopped nuts, to decorate

1 Cut sponge rolls into 1 cm ($\frac{1}{2}$ in) slices and use half the slices to line base and sides of a glass bowl. Sprinkle slices with half the sherry, Marsala or port.

2 Arrange half the apricots on top of cake and cover with half the custard.

3 Chop jelly into cubes and sprinkle half over the custard. Place another layer of cake slices on top, moisten with remaining sherry, Marsala or port. Add another layer of apricots, custard and jelly.

4 Beat cream until thick and fill a piping bag. Pipe cream in a lattice pattern over top of trifle and decorate with fruit and nuts. Chill until ready to serve.

COOK'S TIP

Trifle is always a family favourite, but you might like to make younger children a small 'special' version without alcohol. In this case, simply sprinkle the cake layers with juice from canned apricots, or orange or pineapple juice.

MULLED FRUIT SORBET

SERVES 6

2 teaspoons powdered gelatine
500 g (1 lb) mixture of soft fruits such as apricots, peaches, plums, raspberries, blackberries, strawberries
1 clementine
14 whole cloves
2 cinnamon sticks, halved
grated rind and juice of 1 orange
250 g (8 oz) caster sugar
300 ml (½ pint) red wine
shredded orange rind, to decorate

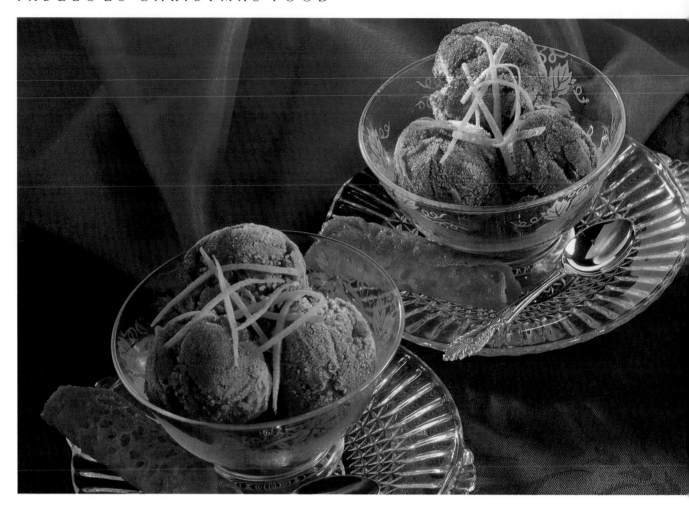

1 In a small bowl, sprinkle gelatine over 1 tablespoon water.
2 If necessary, remove stones from fruits. Put all fruits in a saucepan. Stud clementine with cloves and add to pan with cinnamon, orange rind and juice, sugar and wine.
3 Bring just to the boil. Reduce heat, cover and simmer very gently for 10 minutes. Remove from heat and leave to cool.
4 Remove clementine and cinnamon, then blend fruits and liquid in a food processor. Press through a sieve to remove pips then turn into a freezer container. Freeze for about 1 hour, until firm around edges.
5 Turn mixture into a bowl and whisk until paler in colour and smooth. Return to the freezer, until almost firm.
6 Whisk and once more freeze until firm.
7 Transfer sorbet to fridge 30 minutes before serving. Scoop sorbet into glasses and decorate with the shredded orange rind.

COOK'S TIPS

This is a perfect dessert for a celebration dinner as it can be made well in advance. Both the Apricot Sauce on page 65 and the Chocolate Sauce on page 61, served chilled, contrast pleasantly with it but for a more elaborate presentation, serve scoops on to a pool of fruit sauce (see Sweet Sauces on page 61). For convenience, scoops can be arranged on a tray in a single layer and returned to the freezer until ready to serve.

CHRISTMAS ALASKA

SERVES 8

1 luxury Swiss roll
1.1 litre (1¾ pints) dairy vanilla ice cream
1 individual Christmas pudding, weighing about 180 g (6 oz)
2 tablespoons rum
4 egg whites
250 g (8 oz) caster sugar
icing sugar, for dusting
holly leaves and glacé fruits, to decorate

★

1 Slice the Swiss roll and arrange tightly in the base of an 18 cm (7 in) round loose-bottomed cake [illegible] trimmings to fill [illegible]

2 Turn ice cream into a bowl and break up. Leave for 10–15 minutes to soften slightly.

3 Crumble the Christmas pudding then beat it, with the rum, into the ice cream until fairly evenly incorporated. Spoon over the sponge and lightly pack down. Chill in the freezer overnight or until completely firm.

4 Whisk egg whites until stiff. Gradually add sugar, a tablespoon at a time, whisking well after each addition until stiff and glossy.

5 Lift the ice cream out of tin and slide on to an ovenproof dish. (A flan dish or base of a flan tin is ideal). Cover completely with the meringue, spreading evenly over surface with a palette knife and lifting it attractively into peaks. Return to the freezer until ready to serve.

6 Preheat oven to 230C (450F/Gas 8). Bake Alaska for 3–4 minutes, watching closely, until peaks are turning golden. Dust with icing sugar. Surround with holly and glacé fruits and serve immediately.

COOK'S TIPS

Many variations can be made of this festive favourite. You could use a sponge flan case for the base and this could be sprinkled with a little rum, brandy or orange flavoured liqueur. The ice cream too, could be flavoured with a liqueur.

When covering the ice cream with the meringue, make sure it's completely coated. It's this that stops the ice cream from melting, even at such a high oven temperature.

RATAFIA AND MUSCOVADO TRIFLE

SERVES 8

1 kg (2 lb) apricots or sweet plums
315 g (10 oz) ratafia biscuits
5 tablespoons medium sherry
600 ml (1 pint) double cream
250 g (8 oz) Greek yogurt
1 teaspoon vanilla essence
60 g (2 oz) dark muscovado sugar

1 Halve and remove stones from the apricots or plums. Put in a saucepan with 150 ml ($\frac{1}{4}$ pint) boiling water. Cover pan with a tight fitting lid and cook fruit for about 3 minutes until slightly softened. Drain and leave to cool.

2 Reserve a few of the biscuits. Place remainder in a large glass serving bowl or 8 tall serving glasses. Pour the sherry over the biscuits then add the cooled fruit.

3 Whip cream until just beginning to stand in peaks. Stir in the yogurt and vanilla essence. Spread a quarter of the cream over the fruits and sprinkle with half the sugar. Spoon over another quarter of the cream and sprinkle with remaining sugar.

4 Pile spoonfuls of remaining cream in centre of trifle. Lightly crush reserved biscuits and scatter over the trifle. Chill for several hours or overnight, to allow the sugar to dissolve, before serving.

COOK'S TIPS

Sprinkle the muscovado sugar right to the edges of the dish or glasses so that it looks attractive as it dissolves into the cream. It is important to chill the trifle before serving to let the flavours mingle. Leave for at least several hours or overnight, during which time the sugar will dissolve, giving the trifle a lovely colour and taste.

If liked, the trifle can be topped with toasted almonds. Spread flaked almonds on a piece of foil and place under the grill. Cook until golden brown, turning the almonds frequently. Leave cool before

Clementines
with Whipped Rosemary Cream

SERVES 8

300 ml (½ pint) double cream
5 sprigs of rosemary
1 tablespoon icing sugar
1.5 kg (3 lb) clementines
375 g (12 oz) caster sugar
5 tablespoons Cointreau or Grand Marnier
rosemary sprigs and bay leaves, to decorate

1 Put 150 ml (¼ pint) of the cream in a saucepan with the rosemary

Remove from the heat and leave for 20 minutes or until cooled. Strain the cream into a bowl and add remaining cream and icing sugar. Whip until just beginning to stand in peaks. Transfer to a serving dish and chill.
2 Peel clementines and prick all over with a fork. Place in a glass serving dish.
3 Put sugar and 100 ml (4fl oz) water in a heavy-based saucepan and heat gently, until dissolved. Bring to the boil and boil, without stirring, until syrup turns to a golden caramel.
4 Place base of pan into cold water to prevent further cooking. Add 450 ml (¾ pint) boiling water to pan and return to heat until caramel has dissolved.
5 Leave until cold then add liqueur and pour over the clementines. Chill for several hours or overnight. Decorate with herbs and serve with the whipped cream.

Cook's Tip
If making a day in advance, prepare the whipped cream nearer serving time as it will become very thick if left overnight.

Chocolate Cream Truffles

MAKES ABOUT 18

180 g (6 oz) plain chocolate
60 g (2 oz) white chocolate
100 ml (4fl oz) double cream
1 tablespoon brandy or rum
cocoa powder, for dusting

★

1 Break the plain chocolate and white chocolate, separately, into squares. Pour cream into a saucepan and bring almost to the boil. Remove from the heat and stir in 125 g (4 oz) of the plain chocolate.

2 Stir frequently until the chocolate has melted. Stir in brandy or rum and turn into a bowl. Leave to cool then chill in the refrigerator until mixture is completely cold.

3 Using an electric whisk, beat until paler in colour and just firm. Take teaspoonfuls of the mixture and shape into balls. Chill for 30 minutes.

4 Put remaining plain chocolate in a bowl and stand over a pan of simmering water until melted. Melt white chocolate in the same way. Leave to cool slightly.

5 Line a tray with greaseproof paper. Using two forks, dip a truffle in the plain chocolate then transfer to the tray. Lightly fork the surface to give it texture.

6 Coat a third of the truffles in the plain chocolate and a third in the white chocolate. Roll remaining truffles in the cocoa.

7 Store in refrigerator for up to 4 days. Serve in petit four cases.

Chocolate Hazelnut Layers

SERVES 12

rice paper, for lining tin
60 g (2 oz) glacé pineapple
200 g (7 oz) plain chocolate
200 g (7 oz) white chocolate
finely grated rind of 1 orange
1 tablespoon Cointreau or orange liqueur
60 g (2 oz) hazelnuts

1 Line an 18 cm (6 in) round cake tin with rice paper, as you would with greaseproof paper, letting rice paper come 1 cm (½ in) up sides of tin. Chop the pineapple.

2 Break

squares and put in a bowl. Stand bowl over a saucepan of simmering water and leave until melted.

3 Spread half the plain chocolate over base of lined tin. Chill until beginning to harden.

4 Break white chocolate into squares and put in a bowl with the orange rind and liqueur. Melt, stirring, until only just combined as the chocolate will quickly solidify.

5 Spread the melted white chocolate over the dark chocolate layer then cover with remaining plain chocolate.

6 Immediately scatter the glacé pineapple and hazelnuts over the chocolate, then press down into chocolate until almost submerged. Chill for at least 1 hour.

Serve cut into 12 wedges.

CHOCOLATE COFFEE CUPS

MAKES 12

410 g (13 oz) plain chocolate
200 g (7 oz) cream cheese
$\frac{1}{2}$ teaspoon vanilla essence
1 tablespoon coffee, made from expresso ground beans
2 tablespoons Tia Maria or other coffee liqueur
icing sugar and cocoa powder, to dust

1 Break 200 g (7 oz) of the chocolate into squares and put in a bowl. Stand over a saucepan of simmering water until melted.

2 Mark six 14 × 10 cm ($5\frac{1}{2}$ × 4 in) rectangles on greaseproof paper. Use a palette knife to cover rectangles with the melted chocolate, spreading the chocolate so that it forms a wavy line along each long edge.

3 Leave on a cool surface until just beginning to harden, then cut through each rectangle lengthways. When almost solid, but still flexible, peel off 1 strip of chocolate and fold into a case with straight edge on the bottom, taking care not to break the chocolate as you fold it. Repeat with the remaining chocolate pieces and chill.

4 Break remaining chocolate into a bowl and stand over simmering water until melted. Beat cheese in a bowl with vanilla, coffee and liqueur. Stir in melted chocolate, then spoon into the chocolate cups. Chill until needed.

5 Dust generously with icing sugar and cocoa before serving.

CHRISTMAS TEA

RIBBONS AND STARS CAKE

SERVES 25–30

CAKE

200 g (6½ oz) butter or margarine
200 g (6½ oz) dark muscovado sugar
3 eggs
250 g (8 oz) plain flour
2 teaspoons ground mixed spice
125 g (4 oz) Brazil nuts
875 g (1¾ lb) mixed dried fruit
125 g (4 oz) glacé cherry pieces

TO FINISH

6 tablespoons brandy, rum or sherry
30.5 cm (12 in) round gold cake board
4 tablespoons apricot jam
125 g (4 oz) icing sugar, plus extra for dusting
1 kg (2 lb) almond paste
1.2 kg (2½ lb) sugarpaste
cornflour, for dusting
3 metres ribbon, about 4 cm (1½ in) wide, in 3 contrasting shades
6 lengths fine floristy wire

1 Grease and line a 20 cm (8 in) round cake tin. Preheat oven to 140C (275F/Gas 1).

2 Soften the butter or margarine in a large bowl. Add the sugar and beat together until light and fluffy. Gradually beat in the eggs, adding a little of the flour to prevent curdling.

3 Sift together flour and spice and fold into creamed mixture. Roughly chop nuts and fold in with the dried fruits and cherries.

4 Turn into prepared tin and level surface. Bake for 3–3¼ hours or until firm and a skewer, inserted into a centre, comes out clean. Leave to cool in tin.

5 Remove from tin and remove paper. Prick cake with a fine skewer and drizzle with the liqueur. Wrap in several layers of greaseproof paper and then in a double thickness of foil. Store in an airtight tin for at least one month to mature before decorating.

6 About 2 weeks before Christmas, cover the cake. Place cake on board. Heat the jam with 1 tablespoon water then press through a sieve. Brush over cake.

7 Dust surface with icing sugar and roll out the almond paste to a 30 cm (12 in) round. Lift over cake and press around the sides, easing to fit. Trim off excess paste around the base.

8 Lightly knead 1 kg (2 lb) of the sugarpaste and roll out, on a surface dusted with icing sugar, to a 30 cm (12 in) round. Lift over cake, easing to fit around sides and trim off excess. Using your hands dusted with cornflour, smooth out creases.

9 To decorate cake, cut ribbons into 25 cm (10 in) lengths. Fold a piece of ribbon in half and twist into loops with short lengths of floristry wire. Repeat with remaining ribbon.

10 Using your hands, dusted with cornflour, roll some of the remaining sugarpaste into baubles, about 2 cm (¾ in) in diameter. On a surface dusted with cornflour, thinly roll out the remaining sugarpaste. Cut out about 12 stars using a small cutter or by cutting out 4 cm (1½ in) circles then cutting out points with a knife. Transfer stars and baubles to a piece of baking parchment and leave for 24 hours.

11 Press wired ribbons into cake, mixing up the different colours.

12 Beat the 125 g (4 oz) icing sugar with a little water to make a paste that thickly covers the back of the spoon.

14 Using the icing as glue, secure the stars and baubles around the cake. The baubles look effective if arranged in small clusters.

15 Leave to dry completely then cover loosely with foil and store in a cool, dry place for up to 2 weeks.

COOK'S TIPS

For those who find icing too sweet, a rich fruit cake can be covered instead with a stunning selection of glacé fruits and nuts. Choose from sliced citrus fruits, apples, pears, plums, walnuts, pecans or Brazil nuts. Arrange attractively over the cake, securing with melted apricot jam. The sides of the cake can be decorated with almond paste or simply a wide, festive ribbon. See the Glazed Christmas Cake on page 77 for a more formal arrangement.

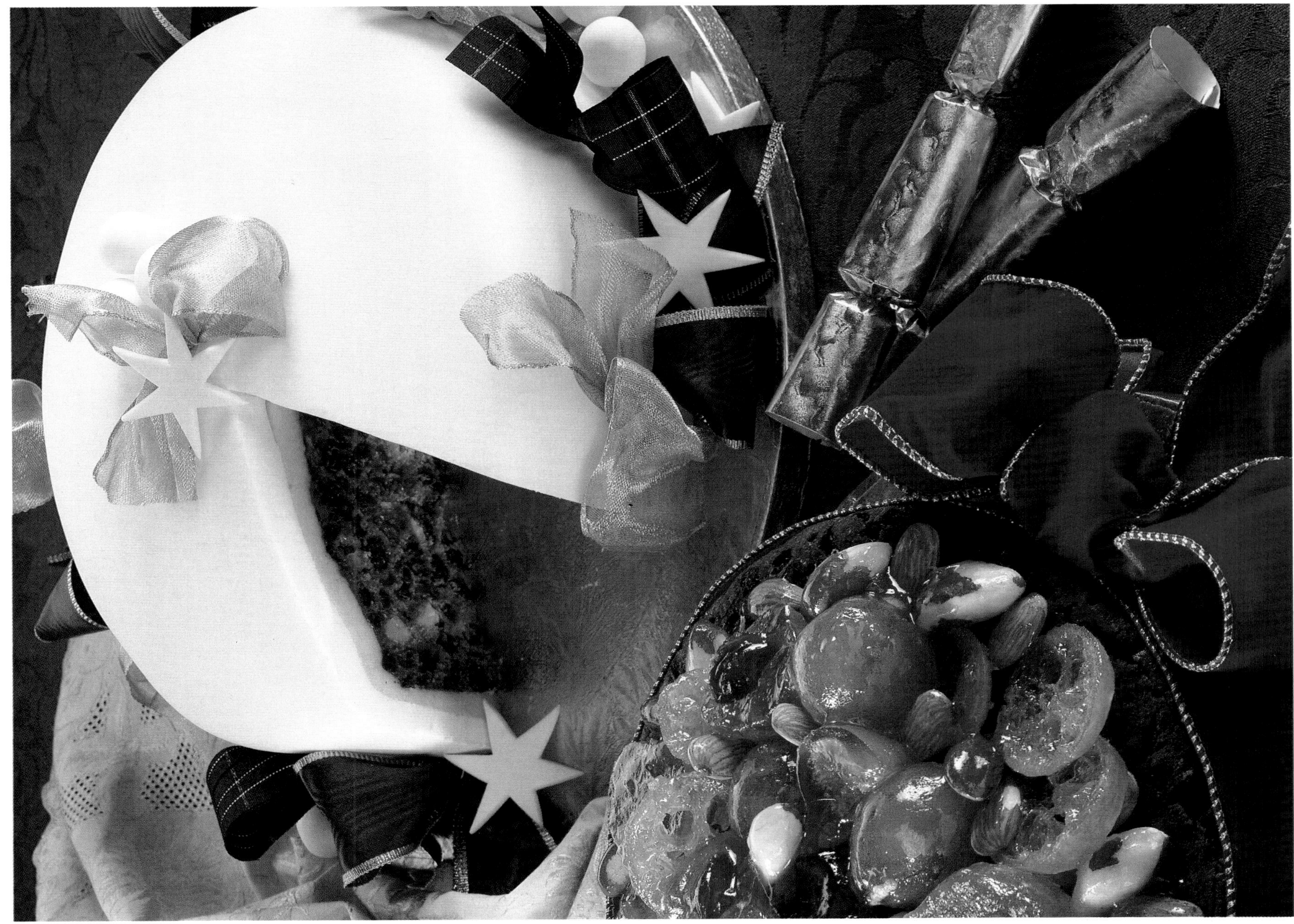

GLAZED CHRISTMAS CAKE

Topped with fruit and nuts, this cake makes the perfect alternative to a traditional iced Christmas cake.

SERVES 25–30

250 g (8 oz) sultanas
250 g (8 oz) currants
250 g (8 oz) raisins
125 g (4 oz) chopped dried mixed peel
250 g (8 oz) glacé cherries
60 g (2 oz) glacé pineapple
60 g (2 oz) dates
4 tablespoons brandy
60 g (2 oz) dark chocolate
250 g (8 oz) butter or margarine
155 g (5 oz) soft light brown sugar
5 eggs
1 teaspoon vanilla essence
1 teaspoon almond essence
2 teaspoons glycerine
2 teaspoons raspberry jam
finely grated rind and juice of 1 lemon
250 g (8 oz) plain flour
1 teaspoon mixed spice
1 teaspoon ground ginger
¼ teaspoon salt
extra 2 tablespoons brandy

TO DECORATE

2 tablespoons apricot jam, boiled and sieved
a selection of whole nuts and red and green cherries

★

1 Grease and line a 20 cm (8 in) round or square cake tin. Place sultanas, currants, raisins and mixed peel in a bowl. Cut cherries, pineapple and dates into small pieces with kitchen scissors and add to the bowl. Toss fruits together with the brandy. Cover and set aside overnight.

2 Preheat oven to 150C (300F/ Gas 2). Break chocolate into squares and put in a bowl. Stand over a saucepan of simmering water until melted. Leave to cool. Beat butter or margarine in a large bowl until softened. Add brown sugar and beat until light and fluffy. This will take about 5 minutes with an electric mixer. Add eggs one at a time, beating well after each addition. Stir in melted chocolate, vanilla and almond essences, glycerine, raspberry jam and finely grated lemon rind and juice.

3 Sift together flour, mixed spice, ginger and salt. Add dry ingredients to the creamed mixure alternately with the soaked fruit, ending with flour. Mix ingredients together well.

4 Spoon mixture into the prepared tin and smooth top with back of a spoon. Lift tin and allow to drop on a flat surface to break up any air bubbles. Bake for 3–3½ hours, or until firm and a skewer, inserted into the centre comes out clean.

5 Remove from oven. Prick cake with a fine skewer and drizzle with the extra 2 tablespoons of brandy. Cool cake in tin on a wire rack, then turn cake out of tin. Wrap in several layers of greaseproof paper and then in a double thickness foil. Store in an airtight container.

6 When ready to decorate, brush top of cake with apricot jam and arrange nuts and cherries as shown opposite.

COOK'S TIP

For a less formal arrangement, see the cake on p. 75.

STEP 1

STEP 2

STEP 3

STEP 4

TRADITIONAL CHOCOLATE LOG

SERVES 10–12

SPONGE

60 g (2 oz) plain flour
$\frac{1}{2}$ teaspoon baking powder
$\frac{1}{4}$ teaspoon salt
60 g (2 oz) dark chocolate
4 eggs
185 g (6 oz) caster sugar
1 teaspoon vanilla essence
2 tablespoons warm water
$\frac{1}{4}$ teaspoon bicarbonate of soda
icing sugar

BUTTERCREAM

185 g (6 oz) butter
500 g (1 lb) icing sugar
4 tablespoons cocoa powder
2–3 tablespoons milk

★

1 Lightly grease a 30 × 25 cm (12 × 10 in) Swiss roll tin. Cut a rectangle of greaseproof paper or non-stick baking paper about 3 cm ($1\frac{1}{2}$ in) wider all around than the tin. Cut slits 2 cm ($\frac{3}{4}$ in) long in each corner of the paper. Fit into the tin, tucking corners under so they fit neatly. If using greaseproof paper, grease lightly.

2 Preheat oven to 200C (400F/Gas 6). Sift flour, baking powder and salt onto a sheet of greaseproof paper and set aside. Break chocolate into squares and put in a bowl. Stand over a saucepan of simmering water until melted. Set aside. Place eggs and sugar in a large mixing bowl and beat at high speed with an electric whisk for about 5 minutes, until thick and light. The mixture should be thick enough to leave a trail when beaters are lifted.

3 Add the sifted flour and vanilla essence all at once and fold in gently and quickly with a metal spoon. Add water and bicarbonate of soda to melted chocolate and stir until thick and smooth. Pour chocolate into egg and flour mixture. Fold in with a metal spoon until ingredients are just combined. Do not beat mixture.

4 Pour mixture into the prepared tin and shake gently so it reaches into the corners. Bake for 15 minutes, or until cake springs back when lightly touched with fingers. Remove cake from oven and turn out onto a clean tea-towel which has been sprinkled thickly with icing sugar.

5 Peel off the lining paper and trim crisp edges of cake with a sharp knife.

6 Fold the hem of the tea-towel over the short edge of the cake and roll up cake, using the tea-towel to help roll. Place roll on a wire rack and leave until completely cold.
7 For the buttercream, beat butter in a bowl until soft and light. Sift icing sugar and cocoa into butter. Beat until mixure is smooth and creamy. Add milk and beat until combined. Carefully unroll the cake and spread quickly with half the buttercream. Roll up again.
8 Cut two 1 cm ($\frac{1}{2}$in) slices on the slant from the cake and arrange on top to resemble a gnarled log. Frost entire cake with remaining buttercream and use a fork to make whorls and lines resembling bark. Chill cake until ready to serve and decorate with a sprig of holly.

STEP 1

STEP 2

STEP 3

STEP 4

STEP 5

STEP 6

STEP 8

COOK'S TIP

Despite its delicate texture and creamy frosting, the cake may be frozen up to 3 weeks ahead of serving. After filling and frosting, place on a tray and freeze until hard, then wrap in freezer wrap. It will take only 30 minutes or so to thaw at room temperature. For a pretty effect when serving, the serving board may be sprinkled thickly with icing sugar to look like snow. Alternatively you could beat double cream until thick and fill a piping bag. Pipe cream in swirls to resemble snow over the top of the log. Add a little Santa and other Christmas figures if you wish.

STOLLEN

SERVES 8–10

125 g (4 oz) butter
375 g (12 oz) strong white flour
good pinch of salt
60 g (2 oz) caster sugar
2 teaspoons easy-blend dried yeast
150 ml ($\frac{1}{4}$ pint) milk
1 egg, beaten
30 g (1 oz) glacé cherries
60 g (2 oz) currants
60 g (2 oz) sultanas
60 g (2 oz) raisins
30 g (1 oz) mixed peel
30 g (1 oz) chopped mixed nuts
grated rind of 1 lemon
180 g (6 oz) almond paste
icing sugar, for dusting

1 Grease a large baking sheet. Gently melt the butter. Mix the flour, salt, sugar and yeast in a large bowl. Stir in butter, milk and egg and mix to a dough. Turn out on to a floured surface and knead for about 10 minutes, until smooth and elastic.

2 Put in a bowl. Cover with a clean tea-towel and leave in a warm place for about 1 hour, until doubled in size.

4 Cut cherries into quarters. Turn dough out on to a floured surface. Gradually knead in cherries, currants, sultanas, raisins, mixed peel, nuts and lemon rind.

5 Lightly roll dough to a rectangle measuring about 25 × 20 cm (10 × 8 in). Using the rolling pin, mark a line lengthways down the centre of the dough. Roll the almond paste to a sausage shape almost as long as the dough. Lay paste down the marked line.

6 Fold dough over the paste to enclose. Transfer to the prepared baking sheet. Cover loosely with a clean tea-towel and leave dough in a warm place for about 45 minutes, until the dough has doubled in size.

7 Preheat oven to 190C (375F/Gas 5). Bake for about 35 minutes until golden and hollow sounding when tapped on underside. Transfer to a wire rack to cool. Serve generously dusted with icing sugar.

8 Store the Stollen in an airtight tin for up to 3 days.

STOLLEN

This is a festive German yeast cake encasing a filling of almond paste. It freezes well and makes an attractive present, sealed in cellophane and tied with ribbon.

MINCE PIES

MAKES 18

250 g (8 oz) plain flour
pinch of salt
60 g (2 oz) butter or margarine
60 g (2 oz) lard
60 g (2 oz) almond paste
375 g (12 oz) mincemeat
grated rind of 2 lemons
beaten egg, to glaze
caster sugar, to sprinkle

1 Sift flour and salt into a bowl. Add butter or lard, cut into small pieces and rub in with the fingertips until mixture resembles breadcrumbs. Add 3 tablespoons cold water and mix to a firm dough, adding a little extra water if necessary. Knead lightly, wrap in greaseproof paper then chill in the refrigerator for 30 minutes.

2 Preheat oven to 200C (400F/Gas 6). Roll out pastry on a lightly floured surface. Using a 7.5 cm (3 in) cutter and a 6 cm ($2\frac{1}{4}$ in) cutter, cut out 18 rounds in each size, re-rolling trimmings to make sufficient.

3 Use larger rounds to line patty tins. Grate almond paste. Mix together mincemeat, almond paste and lemon rind and spoon into the cases.

4 Brush edges with beaten egg then cover with smaller rounds, pressing edges firmly to secure. Cut a cross on the top of each.

5 Brush with beaten egg and sprinkle with sugar. Bake in the oven for about 20 minutes, until turning golden. Transfer to a wire rack to cool, dusting with more caster sugar.

COOK'S TIP

It is worth making mince pies ahead of time as they store well in an airtight tin for several days or they can be frozen. To reheat, arrange them on a baking sheet, ready to pop in the oven for Christmas dinner. Allow about 10 minutes at 170C (325F/Gas 3). Pouring cream, brandy butter or custard all make delicious accompaniments. For variety, try different decorations. The pastry lids can be cut with small star, crescent or holly leaf cutters. Alternatively, cut thin strips and arrange in a lattice over the filling. Don't forget to dust them generously with icing or caster sugar before serving.

STEP 1

STEP 2

STEP 3

BISHOP'S BREAD

This colourful loaf of glacé fruit, whole nuts and brandy will become a firm favourite not just at Christmas time.

SERVES 12–14

2 eggs
125 g (4 oz) caster sugar
125 g (4 oz) plain flour
1 teaspoon baking powder
¼ teaspoon salt
375 g (12 oz) mixed glacé fruit such as pineapple, pears, peaches, apricots
125 g (4 oz) mixed red and green glacé cherries
375 g (12 oz) raisins
500 g (1 lb) shelled whole nuts such as almonds, Brazils, pecans or walnuts
75 ml (2½fl oz) brandy, rum or orange liqueur
extra glacé fruits to decorate

1 Preheat oven to 150C (300F/Gas 2). Grease 2 loaf tins about 25 × 8 × 4 cm (10 × 3 × 1½ in) and line base and sides with non-stick baking paper or greased greaseproof paper.
2 Beat eggs and sugar together in a small bowl. Sift flour, baking powder and salt into a large bowl.
3 With kitchen scissors dipped in hot water, cut the mixed glacé fruit to about the same size as the cherries.
4 Add the chopped fruit, cherries and raisins to the dry ingredients and stir well to coat with flour, baking powder and salt.
5 Stir fruit mixture and nuts into egg mixture and mix together thoroughly.
6 Turn mixture into the prepared tins, pushing it well into corners. Bake for 1¼ hours until firm to the touch when pressed lightly with the fingers. Remove from oven and drizzle immediately with brandy, rum or liqueur. Cool in the tins, then wrap in foil and store in the refrigerator. When ready to serve, decorate top with extra glacé fruits.

CHERRY MADEIRA CAKE

SERVES 12

185 g (6 oz) butter
185 g (6 oz) caster sugar
3 eggs, beaten
185 g (6 oz) self-raising flour
60 g (2 oz) ground almonds
155 g (5 oz) glacé cherries, finely chopped

TO GLAZE

2 tablespoons apricot jam, boiled and sieved
60 g (2 oz) glacé cherries
3 glacé pineapple rings

1 Lightly grease and line an 18 cm (7 in) round cake tin. Preheat oven to 160C (325F/Gas 3).
2 Beat butter in a bowl until softened. Add sugar and beat together until light and fluffy. Gradually add the eggs, beating well after each addition. Sift in flour, ground almonds, chopped cherries and fold carefully into mixture.
3 Place mixture into prepared tin, smooth top and bake for 1–1¼ hours or until cake springs back when pressed in the centre. Cool in tin for 5 minutes, turn out onto a wire rack, remove paper, invert cake and leave until cold.
4 Brush glaze over top of cake. Cut the glacé cherries into halves and the glacé pineapple rings into pieces. Arrange on top of the cake and brush with remaining glaze.

COOK'S TIPS

Mixed glacé fruit really adds a special touch to a cake, and although more expensive than dried fruit it is well worth trying. Both these cakes keep well wrapped in foil and stored in an airtight container for up to two weeks.

STEP 4

STEP 5

STEP 6

CHRISTMAS TREE BISCUITS

MAKES ABOUT 45 BISCUITS

375 g (12 oz) plain flour
2 teaspoons baking powder
2 teaspoons cinnamon
1 teaspoon mixed spice
1 teaspoon ground ginger
¼ teaspoon salt
250 g (8 oz) butter
185 g (6 oz) soft brown sugar
3 tablespoons brandy, rum or orange juice
1 egg white, lightly beaten
sultanas, raisins, almonds and glacé cherries, to decorate

1 Preheat oven to 180C (350F/ Gas 4). Sift together flour, baking powder, cinnamon, spice, ginger and salt and set aside. Beat butter in a bowl until softened. Cream the butter with an electic whisk or wooden spoon and gradually beat in sugar. Add brandy, rum or orange juice, then dry ingredients. Stir until well combined and a soft dough forms. Wrap in plastic wrap and chill for 30 minutes.
2 Turn out dough onto a lightly floured surface and roll out with a floured rolling pin to make a rectangle about 5 mm (¼ in) thick. Cut dough into shapes with decorative biscuit cutters.
3 Arrange biscuits on greased baking trays and brush with egg white. Use a metal skewer to mark patterns on each biscuit and decorate with sultanas, raisins, almonds and cherries. Make a hole in the top of each for threading ribbon. Bake for 15 minutes or until firm to touch. Transfer biscuits onto a wire rack to cool.
4 Store biscuits in an airtight container. To decorate, thread ribbon through holes in biscuits and tie to branches.

FRUIT AND NUT CARAMELS

MAKES ABOUT 70 PIECES

185 g (6 oz) glacé cherries, chopped
90 g (3 oz) dried apricots, chopped
155 g (5 oz) whole mixed nuts
220 g (7 oz) caster sugar
90 g (3 oz) butter or margarine
2 tablespoons golden syrup
4 tablespoons liquid glucose
125 ml (4fl oz) condensed milk

1 Grease a 28 × 18 cm (11 × 7 in) cake tin. Spread cherries, apricots and mixed nuts evenly over the base of the tin.
2 Place the remaining ingredients in a heavy-based saucepan and heat gently, stirring constantly until sugar dissolves. Raise heat to moderate and continue cooking and stirring the mixture for about 10 minutes until it turns a dark golden colour and begins to come away from the sides of the saucepan.
3 Pour caramel mixture over fruit and nuts and leave for about 1 hour until set. When set, chop into small pieces using a cleaver or heavy knife and store in an airtight container.
4 Arrange in pretty paper cases on a festive doily.

STEP 1

STEP 2

STEP 3

SHORTBREAD JEWELS

MAKES 24 BISCUITS

250 g (8 oz) butter
155 g (5 oz) caster sugar
60 g (2 oz) ground rice
375 g (12 oz) plain flour
60 g (2 oz) red glacé cherries
60 g (2 oz) green glacé cherries
125 g (4 oz) blanched almonds

1 Preheat oven to 160C (325F/ Gas 3). Lightly grease a 30 × 25 cm (12 × 10 in) shallow Swiss roll tin. Cut butter into small pieces and rub together with sugar in a bowl.
2 Gradually work in the ground rice, then sift in the plain flour, until mixure forms a ball.
3 Press dough evenly into the prepared tin and mark lightly into 5 cm (2 in) squares. Decorate with cherries and almonds. Bake for 40 minutes, or until golden.
4 Cool before cutting up.

Cheese-Pecan Crisps

SERVES 6–8

60 g (2 oz) plain flour
60 g (2 oz) self-raising flour
pinch of salt
generous pinch of ground chilli
60 g (2 oz) butter
185 g (6 oz) grated Cheddar cheese
60 g (2 oz) walnuts, finely chopped
2 tablespoons beer or water

1 Preheat oven to 180C (350F/Gas 4). Sift flours, salt and chilli into a bowl. Rub in butter until mixture resembles breadcrumbs. Stir in cheese and walnuts.

2 Add beer or water and mix to a dough. Chill for 30 minutes, then roll out thinly on a lightly floured surface. Cut into small rounds. Bake on lightly greased baking trays for about 15 minutes until crisp. Cool, then store in an airtight container.

STEP 1

STEP 2

Marinated Mushrooms

SERVES 6–8

500 g (1 lb) button mushrooms
375 ml (12fl oz) water
2 tablespoons lemon juice
60 ml (2fl oz) olive oil
60 ml (2fl oz) cider vinegar
1 tablespoon dried mixed peppercorns
1 teaspoon finely chopped garlic
1 teaspoon caster sugar
1 bay leaf
salt
few sprigs fresh dill, tarragon or oregano

1 Trim mushroom stalks and wipe caps with damp kitchen paper. Put in a saucepan with water and lemon juice and bring to boil. Cook for 1 minute. Drain.

2 Place mushrooms in a jar with a tight-fitting lid. Combine the remaining ingredients and pour over mushrooms. The liquid should cover them completely. Refrigerate for a week before serving.

STEP 1

STEP 2

Sausage Rolls

MAKES 18

625 g ($1\frac{1}{4}$ lb) puff pastry
500 g (1 lb) lean pork sausage meat
1 teaspoon dried mixed herbs
salt and pepper
1 egg, beaten

1 Preheat oven to 220C (425F/Gas 7). Roll out pastry on a lightly floured surface to a rectangle measuring 46 × 15 cm (18 × 6 in). Cut pastry in half to give 2 strips 7.5 cm (3 in) wide.

2 Place sausage meat in a bowl and mix in herbs and salt and pepper. Divide sausage meat in half and shape each half into a long roll.

3 Lay a roll of sausage meat in the centre of each pastry strip and brush the edges of the pastry with beaten egg. Fold pastry over and seal long edges.

4 Brush sausage rolls with egg, then cut into 5 cm (2 in) pieces. Score top of sausage rolls, then transfer to 2 baking sheets and bake in oven for 25–30 minutes until pastry is crisp and golden.

Cook's Tip

Vary the sausage meat filling by adding other flavouring ingredients. Replace the mixed herbs with other herbs of your choice; add 30 g (1 oz) chopped mixed nuts or pine nuts; $\frac{1}{2}$ teaspoon mustard powder; 2 teaspoons Cranberry sauce; or a few drops of Tabasco or Worcestershire sauce.

Party nibbles and drinks

Cheese and Tomato Puffs

MAKES 20

60 g (2 oz) mozzarella cheese
250 g (8 oz) puff pastry
1 egg, beaten
30 g (1 oz) sun dried tomatoes
2 tablespoons olive oil
1 tablespoon chopped fresh rosemary,
oregano or basil
coarse sea salt and pepper

1 Preheat oven to 200C (400F/ Gas 6). Cut both the cheese and tomatoes into 10 pieces.
2 On a lightly floured surface, roll out the pastry to a 28 × 23 cm (11 × 9 in) rectangle. Trim pastry edges and cut pastry into 5 cm (2 in) squares. Prick all over with a fork.
3 Transfer to a lightly greased baking sheet and brush with beaten egg.
4 Place cheese on half the squares and tomatoes on remaining half. Mix together the oil and herb and brush over the cheese and tomatoes. Season with salt and pepper.
5 Bake for 12–15 minutes, until crisp and golden. Serve warm.

COOK'S TIP
Take care to roll the pastry very thinly as they rise considerably during cooking.

Champagne Sparkler

SERVES 8–10

1 bottle Champagne or sparkling wine
1 small glass brandy
thin slices of lemon and cucumber
600 ml (1 pint) sparkling water

1 Pour Champagne into a punch bowl and add the brandy, lemon and cucumber slices.
2 Add the sparkling water and serve immediately.

Gruyere and Ham Toasts

MAKES 48

6 slices of smoked ham
12 medium slices of bread
180 g (6 oz) Gruyère cheese
90 g (3 oz) butter
2 tablespoons olive oil
salt and pepper

1 Preheat oven to 200C (400F/ Gas 6). Lay ham over 6 of the bread slices. Grate the cheese and sprinkle over the ham. Cover with remaining bread, pressing down lightly. Trim off crusts.
2 Melt butter, add oil, salt and pepper and mix together. Brush half over sandwiches then lay sandwiches, buttered sides down, on a baking sheet. Brush with remaining butter.
3 Bake for 10–15 minutes, until golden. Cut each slice into 4 squares, then into triangles. Serve hot.

Parma and Pawpaw Sticks

MAKES ABOUT 16

1 pawpaw
60 g (2 oz) Parma ham

1 Halve pawpaw and scoop out seeds. Cut away skin then cut flesh of each half into 8 cubes.
2 Cut ham into thin strips and wrap a piece around each pawpaw cube. Secure with cocktail sticks.

Chicken Kebabs

MAKES ABOUT 35

3 boneless chicken breasts, skinned
1 small onion
2 garlic cloves
2 tablespoons vegetable oil
2 teaspoons curry paste
2 tablespoons smooth peanut butter
grated rind and juice of 1 lime
2 teaspoons caster sugar
salt and pepper
slice of lime, to garnish

1 Preheat oven to 200C (400F/ Gas 6). Roughly dice the chicken. Finely chop onion. Crush garlic.
2 Mix together oil, onion, garlic, curry, peanut butter, lime rind and juice, sugar, salt and pepper.
3 Add chicken and stir well. Put 2–3 pieces of chicken on to wooden cocktail sticks.
4 Arrange in a single layer in an ovenproof dish and bake for about 15 minutes, until golden. Serve warm, garnished with lime slices.

SPICY FRUIT PUNCH

SERVES 10

1 lemon
1 orange
60 g (2 oz) light muscovado sugar
1 litre ($1\frac{3}{4}$ pint) cranberry juice
600 ml (1 pint) fresh orange juice
2 cinnamon sticks
500 ml (16fl oz) ginger ale

1 Pare rind from lemon and orange, then squeeze juice. Dissolve sugar in 300 ml ($\frac{1}{2}$ pint) water. Add cinnamon stick and bring just to the boil, stirring.
2 Leave to cool then pour into a large jug with the fruit juices and pared rind. Just before serving, top up with the ginger ale.

CUCUMBER *CANAPES*

MAKES 20

$\frac{1}{2}$ a cucumber
60 g (2 oz) smoked salmon
90 g (3 oz) thin sliced pastrami or ham
4 tablespoons mayonnaise
2 teaspoons horseradish sauce
salt and pepper
2–3 black olives
small sprigs dill or parsley, to garnish

1 Cut 20 slices from the cucumber and place on a flat serving plate.
2 Tear salmon and cold meats into small pieces. Scrunch up and arrange on cucumber slices.
3 Mix together the mayonnaise and horseradish and spoon a little on to each cucumber slice. Season lightly with salt and pepper.
4 Garnish each canape with a small piece of olive and herb sprig.

MULLED *WINE*

SERVES 8

1 bottle red wine
4–6 tablespoons brandy
2 clementines
16 whole cloves
1 apple
2 cinnamon sticks, halved
30 g (1 oz) dark muscovado sugar

1 Pour wine and brandy into a saucepan and add 300 ml ($\frac{1}{2}$ pint) water.
2 Halve clementines and stud

with the cloves. Remove the core then slice the apple widthways. Add fruit, spice and sugar to pan.
3 Heat gently for 15 minutes without boiling. Serve hot.

TOMATO AND ANCHOVY DIP

SERVES 8

1 onion
1 red pepper
3 tablespoons olive oil
two 400 g (14 oz) cans chopped tomatoes
2 teaspoons caster sugar
1 teaspoon mild chilli seasoning
50 g ($1\frac{3}{4}$ oz) can anchovies
1 tablespoon chopped fresh oregano or 1 teaspoon dried
salt and pepper
olive ciabatta or crusty bread, to serve
roughly chopped oregano or flat-leaved parsley, to garnish

1 Finely chop onion. Cut pepper in half, discard core and seeds and roughly chop flesh. Heat oil in a large saucepan. Add onion and fry gently for 3 minutes.
2 Add red pepper, tomatoes, sugar and chilli seasoning and bring to the boil. Cook for 10 minutes or until turning pulpy.
3 Drain anchovies and add to pan with the herbs. Cook for a further 5 minutes, until thick. Blend lightly in a food processor then return to pan and reheat, boiling rapidly if necessary, to evaporate any excess liquid. Season lightly with salt and pepper.
4 Cut bread into bite-sized pieces then place under a moderate grill until crisp but not toasted.
5 Spoon dip into a bowl and garnish with the oregano or parsley. Arrange bread around dip to serve.

PEACH CUP

SERVES 8

400 g (14 oz) canned peached in natural juice
125 g (4 oz) caster sugar
500 ml (16fl oz) peach juice
juice of 1 lemon
1.25 litres (3 pints) chilled lemonade
peach and lemon slices

1 Chop peaches very finely and place in a bowl with the caster sugar, peach juice and lemon juice. Cover and chill in the refrigerator for about 30 minutes.
2 Transfer to a punch bowl and stir in lemonade. Decorate with peach and lemon slices just before serving.

STRAWBERRY CUP

SERVES 10

two punnets of fresh, ripe strawberries
90 g (3 oz) caster sugar
500 ml (16fl oz) orange juice
juice of 2 lemons
1 litre (32fl oz) chilled rosé wine
1.25 litres (3 pints) chilled bottled soda water
whole strawberries and orange and lemon slices

1 Hull and slice the strawberries and combine with caster sugar, orange juice and lemon juice. Cover and chill in the refrigerator overnight.
2 Pour the chilled mixture into a large punch bowl and stir in the wine and soda water. Decorate with whole strawberries and orange and lemon slices just before serving.

TROPICAL CUP

SERVES 10

1 ripe mango
1 small melon
90 g (3 oz) caster sugar
juice of 1 lemon
pulp of 4 passionfruit
500 ml (16fl oz) orange juice
1.25 litres (3 pints) chilled soda water
slices of kiwi fruit and ice cubes

1 Peel and roughly chop mango and melon and purée in a food processor, or push through a sieve.
2 Combine purée with caster sugar and lemon juice. Cover and chill overnight.
3 Stir in passionfruit pulp, orange juice and chilled soda water. Decorate with slices of kiwi fruit and ice cubes just before serving.

MIXER'S TIPS

It is usual to stir clear drinks and shake or blend drinks which contain fruit juice, egg white or cream.
Serve cocktails as soon as they are mixed otherwise the drink could seperate or become diluted by the ice.

MAKING THE MOST OF LEFTOVERS

HAM AND MUSHROOM ROLLS

SERVES 4

8 large slices ham
1 small onion
125 g (4 oz) cooked spinach
185 g (6 oz) cream cheese
185 ml (6fl oz) soured cream
1 egg, lightly beaten
pinch of nutmeg
pinch of dry mustard
salt and pepper
celery leaves, to garnish

MUSHROOM SAUCE
250 ml (8fl oz) cream of mushroom soup
60 ml (2fl oz) soured cream

★

1 Preheat oven to 180C (350F/Gas 4). Remove any fat from ham. Chop the onion and cooked spinach. Combine cheese, soured cream, egg, nutmeg, mustard and salt and pepper in a bowl. Place about 2 tablespoons of filling down the length of each slice of ham and roll up.
2 Arrange rolls seam-side down in a shallow baking dish. Combine the sauce ingredients in a bowl. Add salt and pepper to taste, then spoon sauce over the rolls. Bake for 25 minutes. Garnish with celery leaves.

STEP 1

STEP 2

COOK'S TIPS

This recipe can be varied according to what you have left over after Christmas.
Turkey or pork slices make good alternatives to the ham.
The cream cheese can be substituted with Danish blue or blue Stilton cheese which should be mashed well before combining with the soured cream.
Other soups can also be used, such as celery or tomato.

HAM AND TURKEY NICOISE

SERVES 4

750 g ($1\frac{1}{2}$ lb) small new potatoes
salt and pepper
125 g (4 oz) French beans
125 g (4 oz) cooked turkey
250 g (8 oz) ham
125 g (4 oz) cherry tomatoes
2 hard-boiled eggs
8 black olives
$\frac{1}{4}$ bunch spring onions, sliced diagonally

DRESSING
75 ml (2½ fl oz) olive oil
2 tablespoons red wine vinegar
½ clove garlic, crushed
1 tablespoon wholegrain mustard
pinch of sugar

1 Cook potatoes in a saucepan of boiling salted water for 10–12 minutes until just cooked. Drain and allow to cool. Top and tail beans and blanch in boiling water, the refresh in cold water and drain. Transfer potatoes and beans to a large serving bowl.
2 Cut turkey and ham into strips, halve cherry tomatoes and cut eggs into quarters. Add to the potatoes and beans with olives and spring onions.
3 To make dressing, stir all ingredients together with salt and pepper in a small bowl until combined. Pour over the salad and toss gently to mix.

Clockwise from top right: *Turkey Creole; Turkey & Chutney Loaf; Ham and Potato Cakes; Ham and Turkey Niçoise; and Ham and Mushroom Rolls.*

HAM AND POTATO CAKES

SERVES 4

1 medium potato, cooked
185 g (6 oz) ham
2 spring onions or
1 tablespoon snipped chives
freshly ground pepper
60 g (2 oz) plain flour
2 tablespoons vegetable oil
4 slices fresh or canned pineapple
salad leaves, to serve

1 Mash potato and finely chop ham and spring onions. Combine potato, ham, spring onions if using or chives and pepper.
2 Shape mixture into 4 cakes and coat them lightly in flour. Heat oil in a frying pan and fry cakes on both sides until golden brown, allowing about 3 minutes each side.
3 Drain ham cakes. Serve with pineapple and salad.

STEP 1

STEP 2

THREE CHEESE PIZZA

SERVES 6

PIZZA DOUGH
15 g (½ oz) dried yeast
125 ml (4fl oz) warm water
500 g (1 lb) plain flour
good pinch of salt
2 tablespoons olive oil

TOPPING
2 large onions
3 tomatoes
45 g (1½ oz) butter
2 tablespoons chopped basil or marjoram
125 g (4 oz) mozzarella cheese
125 g (4 oz) blue Stilton cheese
125 g (4 oz) red Leicester or Cheddar cheese

1 To prepare dough, dissolve the yeast in the water in a cup. Sift the flour and salt into a bowl, then stir in the oil and yeast liquid, adding a little extra water if necessary to give a smooth dough. Knead well, then divide in half and roll into two 20 cm (8 in) circles. Place on oiled baking sheets, cover loosely with plastic wrap or clean dish towel and leave to rise in a warm place for 20 minutes.
2 Meanwhile, preheat oven to 200C (400F/Gas 6). Slice onions and skin and chop tomatoes. Melt the butter in a large frying pan, add the onions and cook gently for 10 minutes.
3 Divide the tomatoes and the onion mixture between the two pizza bases. Sprinkle each with basil or marjoram. Slice mozzarella cheese, crumble blue Stilton and grate red Leicester or Cheddar Cheese. Arrange cheese on top of pizzas and bake in oven for 25–30 minutes.

STILTON AND WATERCRESS TART

SERVES 4

PASTRY
250 g (8 oz) plain flour
pinch of salt
125 g (4 oz) butter or margarine
about 3 tablespoons cold water

FILLING
2 bunches watercress
315 g (10 oz) blue Stilton cheese
30 g (1 oz) butter
3 eggs
155 ml (5fl oz) single cream
salt and pepper
salad leaves and radishes, to serve

1 Preheat oven to 200C (400F/Gas 6). To make pastry, sift flour and salt into a large bowl. Rub in butter or margarine until the mixture resembles breadcrumbs. Add the water and mix to a firm dough.
2 Roll out pastry on a lightly floured surface and use to line an oiled 20 cm (8 in) flan tin. Prick base and chill for 15 minutes, then bake blind in over for 10–12 minutes. Lower oven temperature to 180C (350F/Gas 4).
3 Meanwhile prepare filling. Remove stalks from watercress. Dice cheese. Melt butter in a large frying pan, add the watercress and cook for 1–2 minutes, stirring constantly, until just wilted. Drain in sieve, pressing out excess liquid, then arrange in the pastry case. Tuck the Stilton cubes into the watercress.
4 Beat together eggs and cream, season with salt and pepper and pour into the flan case. Bake for 30–35 minutes or until set. Serve warm or cold with salad leaves and chives.

TURKEY AND CHUTNEY LOAF

SERVES 6

375 g (12 oz) cooked turkey
1 small onion
90 g (3 oz) fresh white breadcrumbs
2 eggs
2 tablespoons chutney
90 ml (3fl oz) milk
2–3 teaspoons ground paprika
4 tablespoons finely chopped parsley
cherry tomatoes and salad leaves, to serve

1 Preheat oven to 180C (350F/Gas 4). Finely chop turkey and onion. Place in a large bowl with remaining ingredients and mix well.
2 Press mixture into a greased 500 g (1 lb) loaf tin and bake in oven for 35–40 minutes. Serve loaf sliced, hot or cold with tomatoes and salad leaves.

COOK'S TIPS

If preferred, replace the cooked turkey with an equal quantity of cooked lean ham.
This loaf is delicious served hot with a spicy tomato sauce.

Left: *Stilton and Watercress Tart;* **Right:** *Three Cheese Pizza*

TURKEY CREOLE

SERVES 4

1 small onion
15 g (½ oz) butter
1 clove garlic, crushed
1 tablespoon plain flour
1 teaspoon chilli powder
155 ml (5fl oz) tomato juice
155 ml (5fl oz) chicken stock
375 g (12 oz) cooked turkey
125 g (4 oz) button mushrooms
salt and pepper
boiled rice to serve
cayenne pepper and bay leaves, to garnish

1 Finely chop onion. Melt butter in a medium saucepan and sauté onion and garlic until softened. Stir in flour and chilli powder and cook for 1 minute, stirring.

2 Gradually add tomato juice and chicken stock to pan. Bring slowly to the boil and simmer until sauce thickens, stirring constantly.

3 Chop turkey and slice mushrooms. Stir into sauce with salt and pepper. Bring to the boil for 5 minutes, then simmer for 2 minutes. Serve with boiled rice, sprinkled with cayenne pepper and garnished with bay leaves.

INDEX